Identity

THE KINGDOM WRITER COLLECTION

A Faith Filled Guide to Understanding God's Call to Write

DR. CHARIS M. ROOKS

Sapience Atelier Publishing

The Kingdom Writer Collection: Identity

Copyright 2025 by Dr. Charis M. Rooks

Published by: Sapience Atelier Publishing

Publishing Consulting: Sapience Atelier Publishing & Consulting Division

Cover Designer: Sapience Atelier Publishing Cover Art Division & Aaftab Shelkh

Typesetting: Cali Pettiford (https://inspiredscribepress.com)

Editor: Caitlin Faith Miller (https://caitlinfaithmiller.com)

Author Website: www.drcharisrooks.com

Sapience Atelier Publishing is a division of Inspired Grace Ministries LLC. The Sapience Atelier Publishing name and logo are trademarks of Inspired Grace Ministries LLC.

Unless otherwise noted, all Scripture quotations are taken from the Holy Bible, New Living Translation. Copyright 1973, 1978, 1984, 2011 by Biblica, Inc. The "NLT" and "New Living Translation" are trademarks registered in the United States Patent and Trademark Office by Biblica, Inc.

While the author has made every effort to provide accurate addresses for the internet at the time of publication, neither the publisher nor the author assumes any responsibility for errors or changes that occur after publication.

Library of Congress Control Number: 2025918109

ISBN: 979-8-218-78369-3

Printed in the United States of America

Contents

Acknowledgments

To my mother: When I unexpectedly lost you, Mom, it was devastating. I had not yet picked up my pen, but that loss directed me toward the path I needed to take to write this collection. If it were up to me, I would give it all back in a heartbeat for just one more moment with you. I know you would fuss at me the entire time because you would want me to be obedient to God's calling on my life. So, thank you, Mom, for being the guidance I needed to get back on track and navigate through when I strayed. Just like you taught me, Mom, I will always trust in the Lord with all my heart and not just rely on my own understanding. In everything I do, I will recognize Him because I know He will guide my way (Proverbs 3:5-6).

To my husband, Kent: My love, when I lost you unexpectedly, just a week after completing this book/collection, it was a shock beyond words. You were the one who helped me navigate my grief after my mother's passing and encouraged me to write. You often fussed at me if I didn't put pen to paper. I remember when I told you I had finished the book, you said, "Good, now finish the rest. You have work to do, and people need to hear what you have to say." I was upset because I wanted to celebrate, take a break, maybe even pause writing to focus on other things before coming back to it. Now, after losing you, I understand the urgency of sharing my voice, just as you always reminded me, it needs to be heard in the world. So, my dear, this is just the beginning of what I promised God, Mom, and you I would complete. I am inspired by your love, provision, protection, and encouragement. It was your selfless sacrifice of working two jobs, taking care of me and the kids, keeping our family, and always telling me to keep writing that guided me to reach the finish line. I thank you, my love, and I find comfort in knowing you are with our Lord and Savior Jesus, especially since you gave your life to Christ. I know I will see you again in eternity. What an honor and privilege it has been to love and be loved by you.

Purpose

The Kingdom Writer Collection is a transformative series designed to inspire and empower writers from every literary genre and background. This compilation, filled with invaluable books, products, and resources, seeks to identify your unique voice, activate your God-given potential, and educate and motivate you by offering support and testimonies that resonate with your writing journey in God's Kingdom. Join me on this divine adventure and let your words be the vessel through which God's message is shared, and His Kingdom is expanded. Embrace your calling and discover the impact of the Kingdom Writer Collection, where your writing is not just a pursuit, but a sacred and privileged duty.

— Dr. Charis Rooks

*What a privilege and honor it is to be the pen
in the hand of our Creator.*

Preface

EMBRACING YOUR DIVINE CALLING AS A WRITER

Welcome, my dear friend, to the Kingdom Writers Collection! I'm so glad you've chosen to take this journey with me. While on our journey together, I want to remind you of one pivotal truth: You are God's chosen vessel, anointed to extend His Kingdom through the powerful call and gift of writing. Some of you may have heard someone say that to you, and some of you haven't, but I genuinely believe it holds a special significance for you. God has placed a unique calling and mission in your heart, and your gift of writing is integral to fulfilling that divine purpose.

As you journey through this book, and hopefully the entire collection afterward, I pray that you will find clarity about your identity in Christ, your calling, and the profound need for your voice in this world. Let's face it, we all recognize the challenges life can bring, don't we? The enemy, also known as the father of lies, loves to throw distractions our way. He aims to undermine your identity and sow seeds of doubt, making it hard for you to grasp who you are and the divine mission ahead. This battle, however, is not merely a struggle for words on a page; it's about combating the thief who aims to kill, steal, and destroy your aspirations, hopes, and the divine drive to share your story with the world. The very message that can help others navigate the challenges life can bring. Remember, "to kill, steal, and destroy" doesn't just refer to physical life; it encompasses our callings, dreams, and purposes we all hold dear. The very ones that are attached to the lives of others. Therefore, I want to encourage you today: Look beyond your current life challenges! Trust in God's faithfulness and allow His guidance to lead you toward writing, regardless of the distractions or burdens. You are called to be a beacon of light, full of hope and truth in this world, fulfilling the Great Commission. God has plans for you, plans filled with a hope and a future, as beautifully stated in Jeremiah 29:11.

Now that I have told you a little bit about this collection, allow me to formally introduce myself. My name is Dr. Charis Rooks, but you can simply call me Doc. Like you, I am on this journey as a Kingdom Writer, dedicated to expanding God's Kingdom through writing. Yet I confess that even I often find myself struggling to prioritize writing as God has instructed. There are days when picking up my pen or opening my laptop feels like an uphill battle. As Mrs. Sophia from *The Color Purple* famously said, "All my life I had to fight." This struggle has been my reality, especially in the past year as I've worked on this collection. It's only by God's grace that I finished this book, and I believe that same grace has brought this book to you. You see, even in my journey, I've grappled with feelings of being unqualified, grieving the loss of my mother, failing health, financial hardships, and just one week after finishing this book, the unexpected loss of my husband. But I've learned that it's in our weakness that God's strength shines through, compelling us to step out of our comfort zones and share our authentic stories.

If you're curious about my struggles and triumphs that led to the creation of this collection, I encourage you to look for my companion book, *A Kingdom Writer's Testimony*. It chronicles the experiences that shaped my writing journey as I wrote each book of the collection, and it offers valuable behind-the-scenes insights that may resonate with you on your path. Can I be honest with you? I don't understand your struggles as a writer, nor will I try to convey anywhere in this book that I understand exactly what you are going through, because I do not know you personally. But I do not doubt that God knows you intimately. I carry with me the weight of my own writing challenges, and from those experiences, it has become my mission to help fellow writers connect with God's will through my testimony. I hope that this collection and my testimony serve as a source of compassion and encouragement for you, like a friend sitting across from you, ready to uplift you through those tough moments.

Let's be real: This desire to share with you is a journey that took time to develop. When God called me to write this collection, especially focusing on identity, I felt overwhelmed and consumed with grief from losing my mother. It seemed counterintuitive for me to share about identity when I was battling my questions about who I was while navigating loss. Yet, there was this persistent flame inside me, a longing for obedience to God, that ultimately kept me writing. As I reflect on these challenges, I am reminded of a precious conversation with my mother, where she expressed her pride in my obedience to God's voice. It went a little something like this…

> *Mom: Hey, Meegan.*
> *Me: Hi, Ma. What's up?*
> *Mom: I just want you to know how proud I am of you.*
> *Me: Proud of me for what?*
> *Mom: For listening and following God's guidance, even when it's tough.*
> *Me: Well, duh, Mom! That's what we're supposed to do. It's what you taught me.*
> *Mom: Yes, but you have to understand that not everyone does that. I didn't always make that choice myself, Meegan.*
> *Me: Um, okay, Ma.*
> *Mom: I'm serious. Promise me that no matter what happens, you will always do what God asks of you.*
> *Me: I promise, Mom.*

In the quiet moments after my mom passed, I held on to a promise I made to her: "Promise me you will always do what God says." Those words echo in my mind every single day, reminding me to stay true to my commitment, especially when life gets hard. I made that same promise to my husband, who stood by me during the challenging times of writing this book. While my mom couldn't be there, my husband saw my struggles, my frustrations, and the moments when I felt like giving up. He was my rock, constantly encouraging me and pushing me to keep going. He made sure I understood how important it was to finish what I started. My biggest hope is to be for you what my mom and husband were for me, a strong reminder to follow your call to write and a voice of motivation that pushes you to reach the finish line. I truly pray that my words will guide you and inspire you as you embark on your own writing journey, just as my family's support was a never-ending fountain of inspiration.

Through this collection, I want you to know that you are not alone in these feelings. Hearing God's call to write amidst turmoil is not madness, it's an invitation to obedience. And let me assure you, God will equip you with everything you need as you step forward in faith. Over the years, I've talked with fellow writers who share similar struggles, igniting my passion to educate, motivate, and support those like you who feel called to write. Think of this Kingdom Writer Collection as a mentorship experience. Together, we will explore biblical truths and dispel myths about writing for God, illuminating the beauty of your unique journey together. The structure of this collection is intentional, guiding you through three distinct stages of the faith-driven writing journey. The introductory volume, Identity, is designed to help you discover who you are in Christ and clarify your unique calling as a writer. The intermediate volume, Submission, serves as a practical guide for embracing and responding to God's call to write. Finally, the advanced volume, Deception, equips you to recognize and overcome the enemy's subtle tactics that seek to undermine, distract, and discourage writers. Each stage builds upon the last, supporting you as you grow in confidence, purpose, and spiritual resilience. Identity is the first book that helps you understand who you are, not just as a writer, but as a child of God, and grasp the special anointing God has given you to write for His glory. This is meant to assist you in discovering your true self, enabling you to comprehend how to utilize the incredible God-given gift of writing.

I know you may be wondering whether you're truly a writer; perhaps you doubt your ability to express the desires God placed in your heart. Take a deep breath, my friend. God has intentionally placed you in this position. Your purpose is ordained. You may be happy to learn that writing to honor and glorify God isn't confined to a particular person, genre, or form, it's about being obedient to what God has placed in you. Regardless of where you stand, whether you've written extensively or haven't written a word yet, God has plans for you. Allow Him to guide you in your writing journey. I believe each of us is called to be a lighthouse in this world, paving the way for others with our words. If you've never considered yourself a writer, I invite you to embrace the possibility that God is calling you now. Each of us has the potential to influence lives profoundly, and together, we can ignite that fire within our hearts to write.

Before we dive deeper, let me remind you that you are here for a purpose, "for such a time as this" (Esther 4:14). God has already equipped you to be a literary ambassador for His Kingdom, even if you don't feel like it; that anointing is there and will not go anywhere. Know that the enemy also knows this, and he will try to dissuade you because he knows the impact of your writing can lead countless souls to Christ. So, embrace this calling, it's time to step into your purpose. On the other hand, I also understand the challenges that society's impatience can create. I've struggled with this, too. It took serious reflection and perseverance in my writing to grasp that God's perfect plans unfold in His perfect timing, not my own. Daily, I pray for patience for myself and you, as rushing can jeopardize what God wants to accomplish through our words.

Do you remember the meme going around on social media of the little girl not wanting to hand her bear to Jesus? That is the story of my life. Imagine a child holding a small teddy bear while Jesus offers a much greater gift in His hand. I can picture it now: I think to myself, "Look, Jesus, I have this bear. It took me so long to get it, and I'm content with it. Sure, whatever is behind your back seems nice, but I don't know how long it will take to get that. I'm just happy with what I have." I know that might sound strange. But I believe I'm not the only one who feels or acts this way. It may not be a bear, but perhaps Jesus is holding something wonderful behind His back for you, a surprise you've been praying for. All He asks is that you let go of the smaller thing you're holding onto so tightly. Maybe He's inviting us, His writers, to set down what's in our hands and pick up a pen instead, while we're saying, "I need to be practical; I have my own plans." Yet, Jesus is standing there, telling us, "Just write, and I will give you something far greater than you could ever desire or imagine." And just as God led me to a deeper understanding of this through my struggles, I pray that you, too, will find clarity, trust, and strength in Him. Enough to give everything unto the Lord, casting all your cares upon Him (1 Peter 5:7).

Remember, all you need to embark on this writing journey is already within you. When God instructs us to write, He equips us with all we need. My mission is to help fellow Kingdom Writers step boldly into their calling, and I am thrilled to support you in this endeavor. Ultimately, it rests in your hands. Will you choose to obey God's call? Will you let your writing serve as an inspiration to others, bringing light into their lives through your story? I believe you have what it takes, and I can't wait to see how God works through you. You are part of a profound legacy, one that transcends time and leaves a lasting impact. Together, let's embrace the anointing to write and step into a community of passionate Kingdom Writers. Your words have the power to transform, encourage, and lead others to Christ.

So, let's get started on this incredible journey together!

UNDERSTANDING THE KINGDOM WRITER

Welcome, my friend! As we begin our adventure into the world of writing from a Kingdom Writers perspective, let's first tackle an important question: What is a Kingdom Writer? Listen, I already know you might be wondering, what exactly does the term Kingdom Writer mean? How does a Kingdom Writer differ from a regular writer? Is there a specific type of training or certification involved? Don't worry, I'm here to help! One day, out of curiosity, while I was searching online for something, I randomly stopped and decided to Google the words *Kingdom Writer* because I had heard the term used a few times, and this is what I got:

> *Kingdom Writers are those who are steeped or saturated in God's Word. Specifically, we spend time with Jesus in order to be saturated with His teaching. Furthermore, as we spend time in prayer, we are steeped in the presence of God and listening for His wisdom and direction for our Christian writing.*

While this definition is accurate, to me it made Kingdom Writers sound like perfect people (almost mythical) who never face any challenges in life. It suggests that they have endless time to study God's Word, and that all distractions vanish when they sit down to write. They are also saturated and steeped a lot. I know that should not have been a focus for me, but I was like, *"Really, God, what's up with these writers steeping and saturating themselves like they're teabags?"*

Then I said, *"I wonder if the pen is like the stir stick. Wait, those stir sticks are in coffee, not tea. What the heck was I thinking about? Oh yes, steeping and saturating."*

Needless to say, I automatically disqualified myself and said, *"Well, that must be nice that they have the time to do all that. Unfortunately, I live in the real world, and I have real-life issues that don't allow me to steep and saturate in the teacup all day."*

When I first thought about becoming a writer, I didn't have the discipline the Kingdom Writer definition described. I was kind of a mess, no, let me be honest, I *was* a mess, and I didn't see myself as any type of writer, let alone a Kingdom Writer. I faced a lot of distractions and problems in my life. To be honest, life be lifeing. Even now, there are days when I feel tired, frustrated, or just don't want to pray or write. But I'm thankful that my call to be a Kingdom Writer hasn't changed and isn't based on my thoughts, feelings, or abilities. Reading the Bible, praying, and listening for God's voice are very important action steps to take as writers. However, there's more to what it means when it comes to understanding who a Kingdom Writer is than the mere definition tells us.

When I took some time to think about the words *saturated* and *steeped*, I realized that they describe how we express ourselves as Kingdom Writers. It's like when you put a tea bag in hot water. At first, the tea bag is dry, and nothing happens. But when you place it in boiling water, it gets saturated, and all the flavor and goodness seep out. This is similar to how we should express our thoughts and feelings in writing. Just like the tea needs to be steeped for the flavors to mix well, our words come from our experience, whether good or bad, and should be carefully thought out, poured onto paper, and shared so they can truly connect with others. The Bible teaches us to let our words be full of kindness and wisdom, just like Proverbs 16:24

tells us, "Kind words are like honey, sweet to the soul and healthy for the body." In writing, we need to pour ourselves onto paper, like the tea bag releasing its flavor. In doing this, our writing can be a blessing to others, just like a warm cup of tea (and, of course, a good book and a blanket) brings comfort on a cold winter day. Just as our words can bring comfort and encouragement to others, I began to wonder about the people behind those words, the Kingdom Writers themselves.

I think that others like me who search for the term "Kingdom Writer" want to know not just what these writers do, but also who they are. I remember thinking to myself, *If I can understand who they are, I can find out if I am a Kingdom Writer, too.* Figuring this out was very important because I had this weird desire to become a Kingdom Writer, but I didn't know what to do or where to start, or even if I qualified to be one. Writers often might not see themselves as Kingdom Writers because they think they don't fit the definition. The word *Kingdom* can also seem scary, and I understand that feeling. As it pertains to writing, in my mind, it stood for excellence and royalty, and I did not feel as if I was a representation of either. Instead, I felt so guilty about things I had done and sins I had participated in throughout my life that I believed there was no way I could fit the Google definition of a Kingdom Writer.

If you feel this way, too, here's some advice: If you want to discover your calling as a Kingdom Writer, don't search for answers on the internet. Also, stop comparing your past or current sins with those of others. Many times, you will only find opinions from people, not the truth from God. And believe me, those Kingdom Writers mentioned in the definition above are also sinners. The Bible tells us in Romans 3:23 that "For everyone has sinned; we all fall short of God's glorious standard." Let me say that again: "*All* have fallen short of the glory of God." So, instead of having the mindset of perfection when it comes to being a Kingdom Writer, I suggest you open the Bible. The Scriptures can guide you and help you know who you are as God's child and what His plan is for your writing. You might just be surprised to find that nowhere in the Bible does it say you have to be perfect. Proverbs 3:5-6 teaches us to trust in the Lord and not depend on our own understanding. Remember, God made you His writer, and He has a path just for you, even if you do not understand it!

Now, let's dive into a biblically grounded definition but also a more realistic view of what it means to be a Kingdom Writer across all genres.

A Kingdom Writer is:

1. Any writer who aspires to transform and inspire the lives of others through writing creative stories, testimonies, knowledge, experiences, thoughts, or ideas while being a willing vessel used by God.

"I knew you before I formed you in your mother's womb. Before you were born I set you apart and appointed you as my prophet to the nations." -Jeremiah 1:5

2. Any writer who feels the call to write, respond, and write faithfully while not knowing what in the world they are doing, not sure if they even like it, or why God chose them.

"You didn't choose me. I chose you. I appointed you to go and produce lasting fruit so that the Father will give you whatever you ask for, using my name." -John 15:16

3. Any writer who can trace writing throughout their life and see not just the positive impact it made for them, but the positive impact it has made for others, so they write.

"But you are not like that, for you are a chosen people. You are royal priests, a holy nation, God's very own possession. As a result, you can show others the goodness of God, for he called you out of the darkness into his wonderful light." -1 Peter 2:9

4. Any writer who writes regardless of their life challenges (something that always tries to stop them from writing) in order to be obedient to God's instruction to write.

"Dear brothers and sisters, when troubles of any kind come your way, consider it an opportunity for great joy. For you know that when your faith is tested, your endurance has a chance to grow. So let it grow, for when your endurance is fully developed, you will be perfect and complete, needing nothing." -James 1:2-4

5. Any writer who, regardless of whether they do or do not have a large following or platform, just desires to reach those God has intended their words for.

"Remember, dear brothers and sisters, that few of you were wise in the world's eyes or powerful or wealthy when God called you. Instead, God chose things the world considers foolish in order to shame those who think they are wise." -1 Corinthians 1:26

6. Any writer who consistently hears a still, small voice instructing them to write and does so despite life's challenges and fears.

"Trust in the Lord with all your heart; do not depend on your own understanding. Seek his will in all you do, and he will show you which path to take." -Proverbs 3:5-6

7. Any writer who has a goal to one day hear God say, "Well done, my good and faithful servant."

"I have fought the good fight, I have finished the race, and I have remained faithful. And now the prize awaits me, the crown of righteousness, which the Lord, the righteous Judge,

will give me on the day of his return. And the prize is not just for me but for all." -2 Timothy 4:7-8

So, now that we have a better understanding of Kingdom Writers from a biblical perspective, let's take a moment to explore some common misconceptions about Kingdom Writers. Many people think that to be a Kingdom Writer, you must love writing deeply and only focus on biblical themes and doctrine. While it's true there are Kingdom Writers who write within these topics, that's not the only area God calls His writers to. Honestly, I haven't always loved writing. For me, it was a skill I learned over time, and over the years, I grew a desire to write. You see, I've written books, articles, journals, and blogs that helped form organizations in various industries, like consulting, publishing, transportation, and logistics. In the beginning, I didn't set out to be a Kingdom Writer or to help others, I just wrote what I needed when facing tough times and for business purposes. The real challenge came when I decided to listen to God's call to share thoughts via my writings with the world. I was amazed to see how my obedience led God to use my writing to help others.

Take, for example, the transportation and logistics business God guided me to start during the COVID-19 pandemic. I witnessed how our staff became dedicated to Christ and even got baptized. They started giving back to our community, without me even suggesting it. It felt like I was witnessing an intricate design of discipleship unfold in action. All of this was sparked by me jotting down my thoughts on how to start a trucking company that honors and glorifies God on a yellow legal pad. God took that simple act and did far more than I ever imagined. As you can see, God is calling all Kingdom Writers, no matter their background, to be honest, open, and transparent. We need to recognize that we can't do this without Him. Are you a novelist, poet, songwriter, playwright, blogger, or even someone who enjoys doodling or leaving encouraging notes? Perhaps you've never written before or feel unsure of how to start. Regardless of your situation, if you are called to write, you are right where you need to be. God has chosen you to be a vessel that shares His light in the world, and that's why the enemy often targets the creative minds of Kingdom Writers.

It's important to note that, throughout the book, when you read references to your testimony or story, I am referring to any and everything that God inspires you to write, not just your personal experiences. For instance, if God instructs you to write about a red apple, then that is what you should do. God can use any topic you write about to bring others to Christ. A story about a red apple might seem silly to you, but it can really connect with someone who is seriously trying to find God. This is incredible because God understands their love for apples, and reading about them can illuminate a light that starts them on a path toward a relationship with Him. This is a powerful reminder that God's calling isn't limited by our perspective or credentials. He often chooses ordinary topics and ordinary people to accomplish extraordinary things through writing.

Then there are those who I have met with amazing potential to be writers who feel they need special qualifications, like a writing degree or years of experience, to be successful. While those things are valuable, they are not required to be a Kingdom Writer. As a PhD graduate, entrepreneur, and ministry leader, I appreciate the effort it takes to earn a degree. I know firsthand how difficult, frustrating, exhausting, and demanding it can be, as well as what you lose and gain during the process. But I also know that many people, with no formal training, are called by God to write. I didn't have special degrees or credentials when I began writing. I just had, and still have, a desire to write. This journey reminded me that it's not about having a flawless start, but about being willing to step out in faith and let God work through our imperfections.

Looking back, I can see the mistakes in my early work. At one time, I was so embarrassed that I thought about taking my books back out of circulation and rewriting everything. But then God stopped me. He showed me that those early writings were important for my growth and, most importantly, my story. They showed how He took an untrained writer like me and used my willingness to learn over time to create stories that changed not only my life but also the lives of others. I was focused on being perfect, but He was just looking for my willingness to be an obedient vessel.

Here's a secret: Writing doesn't need to be overwhelming or

exclusive. The key element that unites all Kingdom Writers, including me, is that we simply write out of obedience. When I first started, I wrote for myself, and even though that might sound selfish, God still used my writings to bless others. Over time, I realized I could pray for guidance in my writing. I now ask God what to write and to help me reach the hearts of those who will read my words.

God calls us to write to inspire others, as noted in Habakkuk 2:2, where we are told to "Write down the vision and make it plain on tablets so that he may run who reads it." Every day, I pray that whoever reads my words will be inspired to write themselves. It may take time to reach this point, so be patient with yourself. Your confidence in writing and praying will grow as you spend more time with God, read His Word, and continue writing.

WHO GOD CHOOSES AND DEVELOPS AS HIS KINGDOM WRITERS

For a long time, I thought that writers were these perfect people who spent their days cozied up in their country estates, writing amazing stories while sipping coffee or tea. I imagined they had fancy degrees in English or creative writing. But then God showed me something different while I was writing the Bible by hand. (I share about this more in the companion book to this series, *Testimony of a Kingdom Writer*.) I realized that many of the writers in the Bible went through some serious life challenges.

Let's talk about the first five books of the Bible, known as the Pentateuch. Moses, who wrote these books, had a tough life. He struggled with his identity and faced a lot of challenges from the complaining people God placed under his leadership. It seemed like he often dealt with people who were negative. A bunch of negative Nancys. (My apologies if your name is Nancy!) Imagine finding out you are Hebrew after growing up as an Egyptian. That would make anyone wonder where they belong. What if the people you care the most about and wanted to help didn't trust you, even though God chose you to perform miracles to help them? What about the family you grew up with? God asked Moses to warn Pharaoh, who just wouldn't listen. Pharaoh was like family, so you would think he would pay attention, but he didn't. On top of all of that, Moses had trouble speaking in front of others, and so he battled with the fear of public speaking. It must have been really hard for Moses to write those five books despite all that chaos.

I admire how Moses handled it all because, honestly, I'm not sure I could have done it. I might have started off trying to help, but by the third complaint, the young girl who grew up in Flint, Michigan, and married a man from Memphis, Tennessee, would have said while walking away, "Well, you do you maneeee, 'cause fam, I'm just doing what God told me."

While Moses faced incredible challenges as a leader and writer, he certainly wasn't alone, many biblical writers had their own struggles, each bringing a unique perspective to their words. Take for example Solomon, who was a very wise man, but he let his many relationships distract him. Even with all his wisdom, he ignored the warnings God gave him. Because of the choices he made, he lost his focus on God. There was also the grief he dealt with. In Ecclesiastes 1:18, he said, "The greater my wisdom, the greater my grief. To increase knowledge only increases sorrow."

This really resonates with me. I know what grief feels like, especially after losing close family members. I also found it hard to think about writing when dealing with my emotions. Still, Solomon wrote what God guided him to, even though it was painful for him because of the knowledge he had been given. Throughout his life, with all its ups and downs, he wrote three important books: Proverbs, Ecclesiastes, and the Song of Songs also known as, Wisdom Literature of the Bible. Solomon's experiences remind us that wisdom comes with great responsibility and sometimes leads to sadness, but it can also bring us closer to understanding God's plans for us.

Then there was David, an anointed king who was considered a fugitive and had to hide in a cave from King Saul, writing to God to protect him from his enemies because he was afraid for his life. Can you imagine someone chasing you down to kill you because you are anointed, and all you feel you can do is write songs? Even though he was scared and always looking over his shoulder, David still took the time to write what we know today as many of the Psalms. David's ability to write in the middle of his troubles highlights he was able to connect with God through his words and worship, even while he faced the challenge of running for his life.

So why do we think we need to be perfect at writing, or that we must have a certain level of education or a large following? I just gave examples of three authors, but the Bible has over forty authors, some known and some not. They were all different, yet they wrote powerful God breathed words that impact our lives today while facing their life-challenging issues. And guess what? We can learn a lot from their experiences. Every time we open the Bible, we see the stories of Kingdom Writers who, like us, had their struggles and imperfections but were still obedient to write and share God's message. These writers showed us that we all have a story to tell. Like them, we can share what we've learned and how we see God in our lives. This helps others understand and find hope. If we write, we can help bring people to Christ. But when we stay quiet, we might miss out on how we can make a difference in the world.

As we begin our journey, I want to remind you that throughout my life, I've felt called to many different things. Though this book focuses on writing, I've also leaned on many principles that I share in this book when I've doubted my roles as a mother, daughter, wife, leader, outreach pastor, teacher, entrepreneur, and musician. I encourage you to do the same! Think about the special calling that God has given you in this season of your life, especially during times when you struggle with your identity. As for those of you called to write, remember that your writing journey flows directly from who you are in Christ. You are chosen and gifted to be a writer, just like it says in Romans 1:5-6 (ESV): Through Christ, God has given us the privilege and authority to share the good news with everyone. This is so they can believe and honor Him, bringing glory to His name. And guess what? You are part of this wonderful family of believers included in God's great story.

As we continue this journey together, embrace who you are in Christ and let your writing reflect that beautiful truth!

CHAPTER 1

God s Love

WHO IS GOD, AND WHAT IS HE LIKE?

TO TRULY GRASP the incredible gift of grace that God has bestowed on you as a writer, it is essential first to understand God's amazing love for you. It's unfathomable and unconditional, and it forms the very foundation of everything we know about Him. But to describe this love, we must first clarify who God is. This journey starts by recognizing His existence and understanding His nature. Just like my grandson, who often asks me interesting questions about the Bible, we should also want to learn more about God. Recently, my grandson asked me, "Nana, what does God look like?" His simple question made me think and look for answers that I could share with him. It's important to find answers, and they should come from the right source: the Bible. In Deuteronomy 11:18-19, it says, "So commit yourselves wholeheartedly to these words of mine. Tie them to your hands and wear them on your forehead as reminders. Teach them to your children. Talk about them when you are at home and when you are on the road, when you go to bed and when you get up." I decided to learn more about God so I could teach my grandson who He is.

While I searched for information, I also wanted to help writers understand God's nature and character. Here's what I discovered:

The Bible begins simply, stating, "In the beginning, God created the heavens and the earth" (Genesis 1:1). It doesn't try to prove that God exists; it just reveals that He does. This means that God is the One who created everything around us. The earth, the stars, the plants, and the animals all come from His powerful creation. It's like when an artist creates a beautiful painting; the artist shows us their talent and imagination. Similarly, God shows us His strength and love through the world He made for us. This first line of Scripture invites us to think about the wonder of creation and the amazing things that God can do. Alongside this foundational truth, we learn about God's very essence. 1 John 4:7 tells us, "Dear friends, let us continue to love one another, for love comes from God. Anyone who loves is a child of God and knows God". This biblical truth teaches us that love is not just something God does but is intrinsically who He is. Such knowledge deepens our relationship with Him and is vital for our fellowship, salvation, service, and spiritual maturity. The Bible also tells us that God is love (1 John 4:8) and that He created us in His image (Genesis 1:27). This is a powerful reminder that our creative abilities, including writing, are gifts from Him that reflect His character. This knowledge of God's love and creative intent naturally shapes the way we approach our own purpose, especially as we strive to honor Him through our writing and our influence on those around us.

We are each called to know God's nature and His will. As individuals seeking to write with His guidance, we carry the responsibility not just for ourselves, but, as I mentioned before, to share these revelations with others, especially our children. The Bible reminds us in Deuteronomy 29:29, "The Lord our God has secrets known to no one... we and our children are accountable forever for all that He has revealed to us." God reveals Himself in ways we can comprehend, using imagery that resonates. In John 4:24, it says, "For God is Spirit, so those who worship Him must worship in spirit and in truth." This means that God isn't just a physical being like us. He is not limited by things like time or space. God is infinite, meaning He has no beginning or end, and He is always present. Understanding that God is Spirit helps us realize that we can reach out to Him anywhere and anytime. Because His presence isn't limited by physical boundaries, our connection with Him becomes deeply personal and authentic. When we want to worship God, we should do it from our hearts, and with sincerity. Worship is more than just singing songs; it's also about having a true connection with Him. It's an invitation for us to reflect on how we can be sincere and genuine in our worship.

Additionally, we must recognize that God embodies light and purity. "God is light, and there is no darkness in Him at all" (1 John 1:5). This powerful statement tells us that within God, there can be no sin or wrongdoing, and His love is pure and untainted. He is not filled with hate or anger; instead, He is the very definition of love. The message is clear: to know God is to know love. Much like a guiding star, His character should illuminate our paths as we pursue our dreams, including our writing. As we deepen our understanding of who God is, it naturally shapes the way we approach our writing and the message we share with others.

Understanding God's essence is crucial for any writer, as it informs the way we express love and His grace in our work. God is omnipresent, meaning He is everywhere at once; He is omniscient, fully understanding all things; and He is omnipotent, possessing all power. By knowing God and reflecting on His nature, we discover not only who He is, but also how we can embody His love as we write. When we write with the heart of God, we spread His light, truth, and love into the world, creating stories that inspire and uplift others. This beautiful journey of discovery and sharing is not just about us; it's about revealing God's wonderful truth to everyone we encounter.

GOD'S LOVE: A WARM EMBRACE FOR ALL

God's love is the most fundamental truth in our lives, and it serves as the foundation for everything we do, including our writing. You might be thinking, "I already know that God loves me, so what's new?" It's easy to nod in agreement with a statement so widely known, but I've come to realize, through my own journey, that understanding God's love runs much deeper than just a surface acknowledgment. Even after earning a PhD in Christian Leadership, I struggled with truly absorbing and experiencing this love. I often found myself teaching concepts that I hadn't fully embraced for myself, leading to a disconnect in my relationship with Him. It was like trying to explain a beautiful painting without having seen it; the words felt hollow.

If I reflect on my own struggles with identity, I can understand how some may share similar feelings. Past traumas can create barriers in our hearts, making it challenging to connect with the magnitude of God's love for us. Sometimes, those old wounds whisper that we're not worthy or that true acceptance is out of reach. But when we pause to truly consider what it means to be loved by God, the story becomes so much richer.

Think about it, imagine if you were asked about your wedding day. You wouldn't simply say, "We got married, and he or she loves me." Instead, you'd share a beautiful story filled with the details of your engagement, the anticipation, the vows, and the joy that marked that special day. Each moment would be vivid, overflowing with meaning and emotion. In the same way, if you are a proud grandparent, talking about your grandchild isn't just a quick mention; you pull out countless pictures, share stories of their laughter and milestones, and express how blessed you are to have them in your life. These stories are told with pride, warmth, and a depth that sometimes words alone can't fully capture.

So why is it that when speaking of God's love, we often fall short? Why do we sometimes reduce it to a simple statement, when His love story for us is so detailed and profound? Romans 8:15 reminds us that God loves us deeply, adopting us as His children with all the rights and privileges that come with that bond. His love isn't distant or generic, it's personal, intentional, and filled with grace. Just as we delight in sharing the meaningful moments of our lives, we're invited to embrace and share the fullness of God's love story for us, letting it heal, define, and empower us each day.

As we look deeper into His Word to better understand His love for us, we discover the beautiful truth found in Ephesians 1:5: "God decided in advance to adopt us into His own family by bringing us to Himself through Jesus Christ." Can you imagine that? We are not only loved, but we are chosen, set apart as co-heirs with Christ! This means that we share the same love that Jesus receives from the Father. Just as He is eternally united with God, so too shall we be. As followers of Christ, this understanding must transform our hearts. We need to know that God's love is not just a nice saying, it's a life-altering reality. 1 John 4:16 tells us, "We know how much God loves us, and we have put our trust in His love." This means we need to lean into that love, allowing it to fill our hearts and transform our lives. When we truly believe in this love, we can share it with others. Consider Jeremiah 31:3, where God expresses His everlasting love: "I have loved you with an everlasting love; I have drawn you with unfailing kindness." Yet, if you're anything like me, you still have questions lingering in your mind. How can God love me after all I've done? The answer is beautifully simple: He knew you before you were born. Jeremiah 1:5 states that before you entered this world, He had plans for you, having loved you since your very first breath.

Let's take a moment to think about something important. Many people struggle with the idea that God can love everyone equally. This can be hard to believe, especially when we think about our pasts filled with pain, disappointment, and sometimes terrible mistakes that seem unforgivable. For those who have gone through tough times, felt betrayed, or made lots of wrong choices, it might seem impossible to understand that God's love is unconditional. But here's the truth: God's love is not dependent on your past, present, or future choices or circumstances. Life's difficulties are reflections of a fallen world, not a lack of love from God. I have faced moments that left me questioning His presence and wondering if I truly mattered, but those doubts don't define the reality of His love. As we continue our exploration, it's essential to understand that knowing God loves you is a crucial building block for your spiritual journey and for growing as a writer. Without this foundation, how can we extend that same love to others? Living in the fullness of God's love allows us to pour out His grace and kindness to those around us. We can't share what we don't know ourselves. Writing, teaching, or leading others becomes a deeply meaningful endeavor only when we fill ourselves with His love first.

Every time we write, we have the opportunity to share

encouragement, love, and truth with the world. This could mean writing a heartfelt letter or a touching story. For instance, 2 Corinthians 7:8-9 highlights how words can bring about change, even when they seem painful at first. God's love inside us can translate into powerful messages that impact those who read them. It's essential to feel that love and to know that we can write without fear, understanding that God's love never fades or fails. Ultimately, to know God is to know His love for us. 1 John 4:16 reinforces that all who live in love live in God, and God lives in them. Remember, our love for God is merely a response to His unwavering love for us. When we grasp the depth of God's perfect love, we find the courage to let go of our fears. We don't need to hide behind our past mistakes; instead, we can approach Him with open hearts, ready to embrace new beginnings. His love is a profound decision, and it doesn't require us to earn it through good deeds; rather, it's a gift freely given. I would like to remind you that there is nothing you can do to make God stop loving you. Yes, He desires for us to turn away from sin, but His love remains steadfast. Life may challenge you but never doubt that God is fully present in your journey. You are cherished and known by Him, and you are called to write and share that same love with the world. So, believe in God's perfect love for you and let it fill your life as you express it in everything, especially your writing.

REDEMPTION

God's gift of redemption is one of the most profound expressions of love we can find. In John 3:16, the Bible tells us, "For this is how God loved the world: He gave his one and only Son, so that everyone who believes in him will not perish but have eternal life." This passage beautifully illustrates how deep God's love is for us. Imagine this: as a parent/grandparent, I have two incredible daughters and a grandson, and I often think about how I would feel if someone asked me to sacrifice them for others. The thought feels unimaginable because I love them so deeply. My instinct would be to protect them at all costs, raising questions about why I would ever consider such a thing. Yet, God, in His infinite wisdom and love, chose to make the ultimate sacrifice, giving us His one and only Son, Jesus, even when He didn't have to. This truly speaks volumes about the nature of divine love, it's pure, unconditional, and beyond our understanding.

As I reflected on God's unparalleled gift, I came to understand that His love for me isn't based on anything I've done. It's not tied to my accomplishments or my shortcomings. In truth, if God's love were based on my performance, He might never have sent His Son to redeem me at all. What's astonishing is that God chose to create each one of us despite knowing our flaws and sins. When I breathe in and out, I am reminded that every breath is a sign of His love. He gave me life, redeemed me from my imperfections, and established a covenant with me, reminding me that my value comes from being His beloved child. This realization about God's unconditional love naturally leads us to consider how redemption is woven throughout His relationship with us, offering both a fresh start and a deeper sense of purpose.

The concept of redemption is beautifully highlighted in the Scriptures, particularly in the Old Testament, where we see the significance of blood representing life. Blood, which signifies the very essence of life, plays an essential role in our understanding of redemption. When we join in faith, we not only accept this gift but also allow God's life to fill us from the inside. This is where the miracle of transformation occurs. We become equipped to fulfill our God-given purpose, reflecting His love and grace in everything we do. The desire to be obedient is not a burden, but a wonderful byproduct of embracing Jesus' covenant with us. It's like the seed of faith we plant in our hearts, which grows and flourishes under God's nurturing care.

As we walk in the light of God's love, it becomes clear that redemption is not just a distant event. It is a daily journey of faith, a beautiful relationship with our Creator. Each day, as we choose to believe and trust in God, we experience the joy that comes from knowing we are unconditionally loved.

His gift of redemption isn't just a one-time occurrence; it's an ongoing series of blessings that shape our lives and relationships. Together, we can celebrate this amazing gift and share it with others, encouraging them to discover the warmth and love that God has in store for each of us. In this way, we fulfill the purpose of our existence:

to love and serve God, to reflect His glory, and to show the world that redemption is available to everyone who believes.

SPIRITUAL GROWTH

When someone decides to give their life to Christ, it's a transformative moment that secures their place in heaven for eternity. While spiritual growth isn't an entry ticket, it is essential for those who wish to be true disciples. Becoming a disciple means actively engaging with God's teachings and living them out in our lives. This journey isn't just about believing, it's about putting that belief into action. The Bible emphasizes this in James 1:22, which tells us to be doers of the word, not just hearers. Just as God instructed me to write the Kingdom Writer collection, I stepped forward in faith, leading to what you are now reading. This is a beautiful example of how God works through obedience and action. In the same way, our journey as Kingdom Writers calls us to move beyond personal transformation, stepping into a life of purposeful action and partnership with God, much like the example set by John and other faithful writers.

Let's look at John, a Kingdom Writer whose life was dedicated to sharing the belief that Jesus is the Son of God. His writings went beyond mere words; they served a purpose, a divine mission to spread the Good News. As Kingdom Writers, our role extends to nurturing our readers, correcting misconceptions, leading them in faith, and sharing our testimonies. In 1 Corinthians 3:6-9, we are reminded that while we may plant or water the seeds of faith, it is ultimately God who brings about growth. Our collaboration with Him in this mission unites us as workers in His vineyard, each contributing to His greater plan. Jesus demonstrated the perfect model of partnership with the Father. He stated in John 5:19 that He could do nothing on His own, and that He mirrored the Father's actions. Similarly, as we hear God's call, we need to set aside our personal desires and embrace His will. This process might feel uncomfortable at times, as noted when we hear the words "obedience to God." Our comfort can't take priority over the mission God has placed before us. It's important to understand that God leads us, and our job is to respond and faithfully follow Him.

Faith is a journey of personal transformation. God doesn't expect us to already have it all figured out. Instead, He cares deeply about who we are becoming in Him. Just like God gave His only Son out of love for the lost, we too are called to share that same spirit of concern for others. Celebrations happen in heaven when one person turns to Christ, reflecting the joy the father had over the return of his prodigal son. The Holy Spirit empowers us to be witnesses, while the enemy seeks to distract and blind those who are lost. As writers, we have a unique position: we should passionately work to lead others to Christ with authenticity, free from self-doubt or hidden agendas. This is to say yes and share with others just what saying yes to Jesus means. When we say yes to Him, we are welcomed into a new family, a spiritual bloodline that transcends our past lives. It's crucial to remember our salvation (I'll talk more about this in detail in chapter 6) is a gift from God, not something we can earn. Colossians 2:20 reminds us that once we have died with Christ, we are free from the rules that once bound us. These worldly rules may seem sensible, but they provide no real assistance in overcoming our struggles. Our focus should be on growing in our relationship with God, who calls us to love Him and others genuinely.

Although it's exciting to be born again, God doesn't wish for us to simply glide through life without purpose. Instead, we are called to love others and disciple them. This means sharing the love and teachings of Christ so that others can also go out and spread that message. Human nature might tempt us to cling to what is familiar, even after we've embraced our calling as writers for the Kingdom. Exodus 14:12 recounts how the Israelites yearned to return to the slavery of Egypt. Similarly, we too can find ourselves hesitant to step out of our comfort zones to help the lost. As Kingdom Writers, we each play a vital role as either missionaries or as part of the mission field. We have the opportunity to uplift others or, at times, require support ourselves. If you find yourself questioning your calling or struggling to hear God, remember that tuning into His voice is essential. Spend time in prayer and scripture, and approach your writing as a sacred duty, filled with hope and gratitude. Replace doubt with anticipation, eagerly awaiting the words God wishes to share with you. Listening to

God is fundamental to our spiritual journey. As believers, we join His mission alongside His guidance. Also, dialogue with God is encouraged, just as Jesus had profound discussions with the Father. Remember the tablets that contained the law? They were meant to guide us toward Christ, fostering a personal relationship with Him instead of simply rule-following. The principle of application reminds us to read the Bible and authentically apply its teachings to our lives, rather than trying to make our lives fit into it.

It's easy to enter into a relationship with Christ, but the real challenge arises when we strive to align our lives with His will. Saying yes to Jesus also means saying yes to His Word, a commitment that calls us to action and perseverance. Kingdom Writers, in particular, must cultivate a reverent relationship with God, recognizing the honor and glory that belongs to Him. This journey of spiritual growth is a pilgrimage that involves belief and authentic living, the fight of a Kingdom Writer is to trust in and walk faithfully according to God's promises. Ultimately, our mission is to reach the lost through our writing, shining the light of Christ in the darkness. This responsibility is a profound privilege, and as we embrace it wholeheartedly, we will witness the incredible impact our words can have in the world. So, let us take up our pens, hearts full of faith, and write boldly, knowing that we are part of something much greater than ourselves, an eternal purpose in Christ.

UNDERSTANDING GOD'S GRACE

What is grace? Grace is often described as God's unmerited favor. This means that it is a gift we receive from God that we cannot earn. Imagine a present you receive on a random day, you didn't have to do anything special to get it. Similarly, grace is a spontaneous act of kindness poured out from God, reminding us of His love and mercy. This beautiful gift provides for us ahead of time, meeting our needs through our faith. In our walk as believers, it is vital to understand that grace provides, and our faith is what receives this incredible gift. Both grace and faith are important in every believer's life, especially for those of us who write for God's kingdom. The Lord has always shown us His grace and love. As it says in Psalm 145:8, "The Lord is merciful and compassionate, slow to get angry and filled with unfailing love."

Let's take a closer look at the story of Joseph from the Bible to understand grace better. Joseph faced many challenges, from being sold into slavery by his brothers to ending up in prison. Yet, through it all, he never lost sight of God's presence. Joseph's journey teaches us that even when things seem difficult, grace can turn our struggles into blessings. Although he experienced great hardship, Joseph always knew that God was with him, guiding him through every trial. His life is a testament to how God's grace works even in tough times. When we look to God in faith, we can find courage and strength, knowing that His grace is sufficient for us, just as it was for Joseph. Grace carried Joseph from the pit to the palace. In the same way that Joseph's story reveals the power of grace in the midst of adversity, we as Kingdom writers are invited to rely on that same grace, trusting that God will work through us to impact others with our words.

As writers in God's Kingdom, we are reminded that "the Father in me does the work," as Jesus said (John 14:10). This means that we are not alone in our writing; God is with us every step of the way. His grace flows through our words and inspires what we put on the page. Our writing can serve the needs of others by providing revelation, releasing them from bondage, and offering understanding and knowledge. It is incredible to think that God can use our efforts to bring hope and healing to those who read our words. When we acknowledge His grace, we not only enrich our own lives, but we also touch the lives of others. Let us embrace this gift and allow it to inspire our writing and our journey of faith.

GOD'S GRACE FOR KINGDOM WRITERS

Before the world was even created, God knew exactly how you would fit into the body of Christ and what unique role you would play. It's truly amazing to think about! He placed special gifts within each of us, and as the Bible tells us in 1 Peter 4:10, "God has given each of you a gift from his great variety of spiritual gifts. Use them well to serve one another." For some, writing may come easily, while for others, it might be a challenge. Regardless of when your gift of writing becomes evident, before or after giving your life to Christ, it is a special gift with a purpose. The wonderful truth is that God's grace has already prepared everything you will need, even for future writing projects, so you can create what easily resonates with others. Grace doesn't just stop at inspiring you to write your book. It continues to guide you in what comes next!

It's important to recognize that embracing our God-given gifts and relying on His grace, allows us to walk confidently in our calling, rather than trying to go it alone or shrinking back in doubt. As Kingdom Writers, we may sometimes feel inadequate, but God's grace fills in those gaps. When we doubt our abilities, His grace empowers us to persevere. However, we must remember that refusing to accept God's grace and the writing gift He has given us can be seen as disobedience to Him. It's essential to stay within the calling He has placed on our lives. If we attempt to write on our own, relying solely on our ideas and understanding without spending time in prayer, we may find that the grace we need is missing. It's crucial to align our efforts with God's purpose so that when we stand before Him, we can rejoice in fulfilling His plan rather than hiding in shame for choosing our own way.

The Bible encourages us to grow in grace and knowledge, as stated in 2 Peter 3:18: "Rather, you must grow in the grace and knowledge of our Lord and Savior Jesus Christ." Just as physical muscles grow with consistent effort, our faith muscles strengthen when we continue to obey God's instructions. Grace can be multiplied, as seen in 2 Peter 1:2: "May God give you more and more grace and peace as you grow in your knowledge of God and Jesus our Lord." Take heart, for essential provisions may come from unexpected places. Think of Moses! When he felt unqualified to lead, God provided support through his brother Aaron. Similarly, as you embrace your writing journey, remember that grace can take on many forms. Recognizing this, we see that grace is not a license for complacency, but rather a continual invitation to pursue our purpose with intention and dedication, trusting that God has already equipped and graced us for the journey.

Grace does not excuse us from honoring God with our talents

because we know we are saved and will go to heaven. As Billy Sunday, the Baseball Evangelist, once said, "More men fail through lack of purpose than lack of talent." It's vital to embrace your purpose without allowing impatience to hinder God's grace. He has a wonderful plan for you as a Kingdom Writer. This gift isn't just a coincidence; it's a calling to fulfill a unique role in His story. Many times, we may need significant events in our lives to wake us up to our calling, and God's grace accompanies us along the way. I am here to tell you that you have been graced to be yourself in every area where God has placed you, embrace it with joy and confidence because all you have is all you need!

GOD'S INTERESTS

In the journey of discovering God's interests, Kingdom Writers need to journey deeper into His Word. The Bible serves as a treasure trove of insights into God's love, thoughts, and desires. Philippians 2:19-21 talks about how Paul hoped to send Timothy to visit the believers because Timothy truly cared for their welfare. This scripture reminds us that even within the church, some may only focus on their own interests rather than His interests. It highlights a crucial truth: being a believer doesn't automatically mean one is committed to promoting God's interests. Kingdom Writers need to be more like Timothy and recognize the importance of aligning their writing with God's heart rather than their own aspirations. This is a vital calling that requires intentionality and devotion to understanding what God wants you to write about. With this perspective, it becomes clear that truly serving as a Kingdom Writer means shifting our focus from personal ambition to a genuine desire to reflect God's heart, allowing His priorities to shape both our inspiration and our creative process.

Current and aspiring writers must prioritize the promotion of God's interests in their hearts and minds. This requires a conscious effort to renew one's thinking and seek divine guidance through prayer. It's vital to ask God directly about His desires for your writing. Remember, it's not just about what you want, but about wanting what He wants. In doing so, writers can discover a fire igniting within them for specific topics that resonate deeply. This inspiration often feels as if the subject comes alive, constantly pulling at their attention and stirring their thoughts during the day and even in the night. As they seek God's interests, they might find themselves jotting down notes, waking up in the middle of the night with inspiration, and feeling the urge to explore these topics more deeply. Sound familiar?

So, what can one do to discern God's interests? The key lies in immersing oneself in Scripture, for it is where God reveals His character and will. When writers dedicate time to reading the Bible, they begin to develop a stronger filter for understanding God's intentions in their lives. By believing in the Word of God over the opinions of others, they build resilience in their faith. Kingdom Writers who actively seek God's guidance through Scripture are part of a small, dedicated group. Such discipline and curiosity are essential in a world that often distracts us from our primary purpose. The choice to pursue God's interests rather than our own is indeed a powerful one, a choice that reflects the heart of a true leader. Moreover, writers should be prepared for the reality that not everyone will share their vision.

This brings to mind the story of Moses and the Israelites, who frequently complained even as Moses sought God's guidance. His example teaches us that pursuing God's interests can sometimes lead to dissent among followers. However, the Kingdom Writers who strive to embrace His mission, regardless of obstacles, will find themselves journeying to remarkable places. It is not about titles or experience, but about being part of the body of Christ, all united under the banner of promoting what matters to Him. Through this collaborative effort, unity can blossom in the Kingdom. Recognizing this, we understand that the process of discerning God's interests not only transforms our individual calling as writers, but also unites us with a greater mission, to reflect His image, share His truth, and preserve His works for generations to come.

We must remember that God created humanity with intention, as stated in Genesis 1:26. He designed us to reflect His image and authority, empowering us to share His message with the world. Kingdom Writers come from diverse backgrounds and experiences, contributing to the richness of the Gospel. Writing holds a pivotal role in capturing God's truths and sharing testimonies that glorify His name. The first biblical mention of writing, as noted in Exodus 17:14, underscores the importance of preserving His deeds for future generations. Therefore, let every Kingdom Writer rise up, embracing the calling to write, for it is through their words that God's voice is echoed throughout time.

UNDERSTANDING THE HOLY SPIRIT: YOUR HELPER

Who is the Holy Spirit? The Holy Spirit is not just a force or an idea; He is indeed a person, just as divine as God the Father and God the Son, Jesus Christ. When we think about the Holy Spirit, it's important to remember that He can be grieved, knows our hearts, understands us deeply, and guides us in our spiritual journeys. In fact, the Holy Spirit is described as the author of the Scriptures in 2 Timothy 3:16, where it states that "All Scripture is inspired by God." This means that every word in the Bible is given to us with purpose, teaching us what is true and showing us where we may go astray. The Holy Spirit and the Bible will never contradict each other, as they work together harmoniously to lead us toward truth and righteousness.

The Holy Spirit is often called "another Comforter" (John 14:16), which tells us He is a continuation of Jesus's comforting presence in our lives. In the New Testament, we learn that the Holy Spirit dwells within all believers, those who have been spiritually reborn as children of God. As mentioned in Ezekiel 36:25-27, the moment we accept Christ, we receive the Holy Spirit, who takes residence in our spirits. This is an incredible blessing!

From that point forward, our lives can be directed by the Holy Spirit's wisdom and instruction, as noted in Romans 8:9. Connecting with the Holy Spirit allows us to tap into profound guidance and support. With this understanding of the Holy Spirit's presence and role in our lives, it's important to recognize the unique attributes He brings, shaping not only our spiritual walk but also the way we receive guidance, comfort, and empowerment each day.

Now, let's explore some attributes of the Holy Spirit. First, He possesses knowledge beyond our own. 1 Corinthians 2:9-11 explains the Holy Spirit knows the thoughts and mind of God and reveals them to us. Additionally, the Holy Spirit has a will of His own, distributing gifts according to His design, as mentioned in 1 Corinthians 12:11. He works within us, interceding even when we don't know how to pray, described beautifully in Romans 8:27. It's such a comforting thought to know that the Holy Spirit prays for us! However, we must also remember that the Holy Spirit can be grieved, as pointed out in Ephesians 4:30, if we resist His guidance or choose disobedience.

Another incredible example comes from Jesus's own life. When Jesus was baptized, He was filled with the Holy Spirit, which prepared Him for His ministry. In fact, Acts 10:38 notes that "God anointed Jesus of Nazareth with the Holy Spirit and with power." This means that Jesus, throughout His time on earth, was empowered by the Holy Spirit to perform miracles, heal the sick, and spread the message of hope. During His time in the wilderness, after fasting for forty days and nights, He faced temptation at His weakest point. But instead of succumbing to the enemy, Jesus emerged from the wilderness filled with power from the Holy Spirit. This scenario teaches us that even in our struggles, we can find strength and spiritual empowerment to overcome challenges and temptation.

Today, many Christians may not fully understand or harness the power they have received through the Holy Spirit. It's easy to overlook just how significant this gift truly is. The enemy often uses our vulnerabilities, our doubts, fears, and past hurts, to distract and discourage us from walking in our divine calling. Sometimes, these distractions can make us feel unqualified or uncertain about sharing our stories or stepping out in faith.

But we must remember, the Holy Spirit is not just a distant presence. He is our Helper, our Guide, and our source of strength every single day. Through the Holy Spirit, we are equipped to write, speak, and act in ways that bring freedom and healing to others. He gives us wisdom when we feel unsure, courage when we feel afraid, and clarity when things seem confusing.

As faith-driven writers and believers, our words carry weight. Whether we are writing a book, sharing a testimony, or offering encouragement to a friend, the Holy Spirit empowers us to plant seeds of wisdom and truth in the hearts of our readers and communities. We are not called to do this work alone. God has given us unique gifts, and He desires for us to use them boldly trusting that He will guide our steps and multiply the impact of our efforts.

Let's not underestimate the influence we have through our obedience. When we allow the Holy Spirit to lead us, our writing and actions can break chains, inspire hope, and point others toward God's love. Every story, every lesson, and every truth we share can become a tool for healing, growth, and transformation, not just in our own lives, but in the lives of everyone we reach. In the same way that our obedience allows God's power to work through us, the lives of those who came before us show us what steadfast faith looks like in action.

Let's look at Joseph again. Joseph faced numerous adversities but remained faithful in every situation. He was thrown into a pit by his brothers, imprisoned on false charges, abandoned, and yet he maintained an excellent spirit, serving others faithfully. One particular instance is when he resisted the temptation of his master Potipher's wife, choosing integrity over immediate gratification. Despite being wrongly accused and imprisoned, Joseph held fast to his faith and purpose. I have never read in the Bible where Joseph says, "Well, since I was accused of it, I might as well do it." I like to believe that Joseph decided in his mind to do everything unto the Lord, no matter what was happening around him. I have a profound respect for Joseph; he was a young man who faced his challenges with steadfast determination, refusing to let those trials change his character or drive him to compromise. Like him, we too face challenges that test our resolve, but the Holy Spirit provides us with the wisdom we need to navigate through adversity, just as He did for Joseph.

Ultimately, the Holy Spirit is our guide and helper in every aspect of our lives, enabling us to witness for God's Kingdom. He leads us to make wise decisions and offers gentle nudges when we stray from the path outlined in the Word of God. By staying connected with the Holy Spirit and listening to His voice, we can fulfill our divine calling, write powerful messages, and empower others to grow spiritually. So, always be open to the promptings of the Holy Spirit, and remember that every moment you spend with Him is a chance for growth, learning, and the miraculous unfolding of God's plans in your life!

PURPOSE

In the Bible, we discover a wonderful message about love and purpose through a conversation that took place between Jesus and the religious leaders of His time, the Sadducees and Pharisees. One day, an expert in the law asked Jesus, "Which commandment is the greatest?" Jesus replied with a message that still resonates with us today. In Matthew 22:37-40, He says, "Love the Lord your God with all your heart, with all your soul, and with all your mind. This is the first and greatest commandment. The second is equally important: 'Love your neighbor as yourself." These two commandments serve as the very foundation of our faith. They encourage us to connect deeply with God while also nurturing our relationships with others. These commandments remind us of what truly matters in life, loving God and loving people.

As we reflect on God's desire for us, we see it clearly illustrated in the Great Commission. In Matthew 28:18-20, Jesus gives His disciples a powerful command: "I have been given all authority in heaven and on earth. Therefore, go and make disciples of all nations." This instruction is like a shining beacon, lighting our way. Jesus calls us to share His love and teachings with everyone, regardless of where they come from. Our purpose isn't solely about receiving God's love but also about reflecting that love into the world. Imagine how beautiful and loving the world could be if everyone embraced this command! When we reach out and share the message of God's love, we can create a ripple effect of kindness and care, just as we desire for ourselves.

Now, you might be asking, "That's great, Doc, but how do these teachings relate to my own journey as a writer?" That's a fantastic question! When we choose to follow Christ, our purpose is made clear: We are called to love, worship, and share God's message with others. This calling doesn't just belong to pastors or church leaders, it includes every single one of us, writers included! Writing can be a unique and powerful way to fulfill the Great Commission. Just as each of us has dreams and aspirations, we have different ways to answer God's call.

Think of it as embarking on a journey to a beautiful destination. While our ultimate goal is the same, each of our paths to get there may differ. Some may fly to get there faster, while others choose to take the scenic route. Similarly, we can express our shared purpose of loving God and others in our unique way through the written word.

However, people sometimes mix up the ideas of purpose and calling. While our purpose is clear, to love and glorify God, our calling can take different forms. It might involve teaching, writing, or serving in our communities. For instance, you may dream of writing stories that inspire hope, while your friend may want to write about their personal journey. Both endeavors are equally important! Both can lead others to Christ. Just as God reminds us in 1 Corinthians 12 that the body of Christ has many parts, each playing a vital role in fulfilling God's purpose, your unique calling as a writer is a significant part of this beautiful plan. So, embrace your calling with confidence, knowing it is a way to express your love for God and for others.

As we continue on our writing adventure, we must also consider the responsibility we have toward our readers. As Kingdom Writers, we write not just for ourselves but for those who might find encouragement and inspiration in our words. It's important to pray for those who will read what we write. Are we asking God to help us write so that we touch hearts and souls? This is a beautiful perspective to have. We can seek God's guidance to fill our work with empathy, compassion, and love. Let's always remember the impact our words can have and strive to reflect God's goodness in everything we share. Our writing can become a pathway that brings others closer to Him, offering hope and healing where it is needed most.

As we embark on our writing journeys, we should keep our focus on God, the source of our calling. Hebrews 11:6 reminds us that "it is impossible to please God without faith." Nurturing our relationship with Him ignites our creativity and helps us produce meaningful words. When we rely on God, our writing not only becomes more impactful, but also honors the divine purpose behind it. Every word we write is an opportunity to express our gratitude for being chosen to convey His truth. Imagine being the voice that helps someone discover answers to their prayers! So, let's step into our role as writers who glorify God. Step by step, let's look to Him for strength and inspiration. With every sentence we write, we can shape our stories into vessels of His love and grace. Thank God for this incredible opportunity to share in this meaningful calling, knowing that our contributions could change lives for the better. Embrace your journey and remember that every word you write brings you closer to fulfilling His great purpose!

CALLINGS: UNDERSTANDING YOUR CALL TO WRITE

Callings are truly special; they go beyond mere tasks and can be seen as invitations from God to play an important role in His divine plan on Earth. Romans 11:29 tells us, "For God's gifts and his call can never be withdrawn." This highlights a comforting truth: God does not change His mind about what He equips and calls us to do. When I first read this verse, I felt a sense of relief, knowing that my calling wasn't something that could simply shift like the direction of the wind. Yet, as I ventured further along my writing journey, I understood that embracing my calling also means accepting great responsibility. If I decide not to pursue my call as a writer, I will one day stand before God with the weight of that choice on my heart. The thought of simply saying "I didn't do it" struck me profoundly. I remember concocting excuses in my mind. "But I did write a little, God! You said loving others (regardless of whether I write or not) is just as important, right?" I pictured myself explaining that I wished to reflect God's glory through different actions, not only through writing. Yet, deep down, I realized God already knows the reasons behind my choices. On that day of reckoning, the words I rehearsed wouldn't matter as much as the intentions of my heart. I wanted the joy of sharing what I had created, rather than grappling with regret over lost opportunities. Like Paul in 2 Timothy 4:7-8, I aspire to proclaim my dedication to my calling: "I have fought the good fight, I have finished the race, I have kept the faith."

Each person is unique, and as writers within God's kingdom, we are called to express ourselves in special ways. We each have a calling that allows us to share our voices and contribute to God's story.

Writing comes in diverse forms such as poetry, journalism, screenwriting, and much more. The beautiful truth is that each kind of writing serves a purpose, guiding various people closer to God. As stated in 1 Corinthians 12:4-6, there are "different kinds of gifts, but the same Spirit." Our varied talents play a significant role in God's grand design, showing how vital we are in the body of Christ. This diversity in gifts is where the beauty shines; God has intricately designed each of us with different callings. I believe that as writers, we are instruments reflecting God's hand, helping to illustrate His narrative on Earth. When I finally meet the Lord, I look forward to asking Him where all of His writers fit into His perfect plan.

For those who struggle to identify as writers, it's essential to embrace that calling, whether we do so full-time or as a side project. I juggle writing alongside my responsibilities in business and education, always striving to uplift, inspire, and educate through my words. However, my calling extends beyond just being a writer. I wear many hats: daughter, friend, mother, grandmother, teacher, and leader. These roles change and evolve, but one thing remains true: I am meant to serve as an instrument of God's love and truth. God has prepared me throughout different seasons of my life, from childhood to my experience as a business owner, outreach pastor, and a business and ministry professor, to fulfill my calling. Recently, I felt the call to shift toward writing full-time. Although I cherished the stability my business offered, life threw me a curveball with the unexpected loss of my mother. During that time of deep sorrow, writing became my refuge; I discovered that leaning on God through my words was essential. Through the process of writing, I gained clarity on spiritual battles and found strength in sharing uplifting messages with others.

You might be feeling the pull toward writing in your life, too, and I encourage you to embrace that feeling with open arms. It's important to understand that every calling in the body of Christ matters. Perhaps you think your calling is small or your contribution insignificant but never underestimate the purpose God has for you. Each written word has the potential to change lives, and your willingness to act on your calling can lead so many people to discover God's love. Just like Moses, who hesitated when called by God, we shouldn't shy away from our divine purpose. Can I tell you something? Countless individuals are waiting for your unique contribution to the world. Don't undervalue your calling; it is intricately woven into God's grand plan. The Holy Spirit is here to guide us on this adventurous journey, reminding us that God often chooses the "foolish things" to confound the wise, as mentioned in 1 Corinthians 1:27. In pursuing your calling, recognize that God desires your active involvement. He determines your purpose and gifts; now, it's up to you to dedicate yourself to this task. Nurturing your writing gift isn't just about personal fulfillment, it's about honoring the unique role God has given you and stepping boldly into the journey He's prepared, trusting that your obedience can make a lasting impact.

To grow your writing skills, set aside time to read, write, and learn about your craft. Remember, your writing is a precious gift, and when you invest in it, you will uncover your voice and the direction your words are intended to go. God's calling in your life is continuous; it's not something you can easily place aside. He has specific plans for you that are distinct to your journey and your identity. Ephesians 4:1 encourages us to "lead a life worthy of the calling you have received." So take that leap of faith to embrace your writing calling! You might find that it leads you down paths filled with growth, fulfillment, and service to others, all while expanding God's Kingdom in ways you never expected.

In the end, remember that writing isn't just about delivering a message; it's about sharing the hope and love of Jesus Christ with the world. We are all called to be ambassadors of His truth, using our talents to illuminate the way for others. Your journey as a writer is just beginning, and now is the perfect time to step boldly into it! Let your words echo the warmth of God's love, inspiring and encouraging hearts along the way. Your calling may be the spark that ignites change in the lives of those around you, and who knows what magnificent things will unfold when you answer it. Together, let's journey deeper into our callings and trust in the amazing adventures God has in store for us as writers!

———

CHAPTER 1 SUMMARY: UNDERSTANDING WHO GOD IS AND HIS LOVE FOR US

In this chapter, we explore the wonderful nature of God and the incredible love He has for each of us. We start by realizing that to understand His gift of grace, we first need to know who He is. The Bible tells us that God created everything and that His essence is love (1 John 4:7). Just like a child asking questions, we can be curious about God's character and what it means to have a relationship with Him.

The Bible describes God as love itself, pure and untainted (1 John 1:5). He is everywhere (omnipresent), knows everything (omniscient), and has all power (omnipotent). This understanding helps us, especially as writers, to share His love and truth through our words.

The chapter emphasizes that God's love is unconditional. No matter our pasts or mistakes, His love remains steadfast (Jeremiah 31:3). Many find it hard to believe that they are truly loved, especially after facing challenges in life, but God's love is not based on our actions; it's a gift freely given. His love encourages us to write and share that hope with others, knowing that His love can change lives. God's power is so much greater than anything we can achieve on our own. Your true identity isn't based on what you do or how well you write. Rather, it is tied to the incredible price that Jesus paid for you. 2 Corinthians 5:18-19 beautifully says, "All of this is a gift from God, who brought us back to Himself through Christ." He has now given us the amazing task of helping others to be connected with Him. The best part about it all is that He doesn't hold our mistakes against us. He has given us a wonderful message of hope and reconciliation.

ACTION STEPS

1. **Reflect on God's Love:** Spend a few moments in prayer, thanking God for His love. Consider how this gift affects your life.
2. **Ask Questions:** Just like children ask about God, don't be afraid to ask your own questions about His character and nature.

3. **Write with Purpose:** Use your writing to reflect God's love. Practice writing stories or letters that inspire others and show them the beauty of His grace.
4. **Share the Truth:** Talk to someone about God's unconditional love. Share verses like Romans 8:15 to help them understand they are loved no matter what.
5. **Grow Spiritually:** Take time to read the Bible and learn more about who God is. Look for lessons in your own life that show His love and grace.

By following these steps, we can deepen our understanding of God and use our writing to share His love with the world around us.

CHAPTER 2
Provision

WHAT DOES PROVISION LOOK LIKE FOR KINGDOM WRITERS?

WRITING CAN BE a profound source of provision, not just for ourselves and our families, but also for those who seek the light of Jesus through our words. As Kingdom Writers, it's crucial to understand that we are called to actively serve God. We must have faith that our needs will be met because the Bible tells us that God will provide for us. Nothing can stand in the way of His promises! All we need to do is believe. A wise soul once said, "God said it, I believe it, that settles it." This means whatever God says in His Word will happen because His Word will never return void. Remember, the enemy tries to lead us to believe that God must perform some grand act to meet our daily needs, but the truth is that Jesus has already sacrificed Himself for us, ensuring we have everything we need. When we turn to God about our writing, we must approach Him with the confidence that He will take care of our needs. At times, we may feel uncertain about our purpose or what we should do next, but Philippians 4:13 reminds us that "I can do everything through Christ, who gives me strength." It's important to understand that whatever God calls us to do, we should not worry about our limitations. Instead, we can trust that God equips us for our assignments. If we do not challenge our faith to reach beyond what we think we deserve, we will miss out on all that God has in store for us. Each day, we should lay our desires before God, expressing gratitude for His perfect timing, even when we may not fully understand how our needs will be met.

Did you know that you can openly express your needs to God? When we chase after His plans for our lives, we will find that His blessings will chase after us. It's time to believe in abundance so that we can reach others through our writing. God has established a divine system in His Kingdom so that blessings multiply. Money is merely a tool to help us share the Gospel through our words.

Don't allow the enemy to rob you of the blessings God has set aside for you! Proverbs 18:16 tells us that giving a gift can open doors and provide access to important opportunities. Our lives are filled with seeds of kindness, love, and gratitude, and when we share these gifts, they multiply in ways we cannot even imagine. With this perspective, we begin to see that God's provision extends far beyond material needs, He delights in meeting us where we are, using every act of faith, including our writing, as a way to open new doors and fulfill His greater purpose in our lives.

Provision can come in many forms, not just financial. It is important to remember that sharing your testimony, offering a kind word, and even expressing yourself through writing can create opportunities for provision in your life. As it says in Galatians 6:9, "Let us not become weary in doing good, for at the proper time we will reap a harvest if we do not give up." When you begin to trust God for your needs, even in the small things, you will grow stronger in your faith and prepare for the larger blessings ahead. Your writing can serve as a conduit for God's blessings to flow into your life. So don't hesitate to pray for all you need! God wants you to bring all your requests to Him, whether it's for finances, opportunities, and yes, that includes support in writing and publishing your book. Just like Jabez who prayed for blessings and an expanded territory, we should approach God with our desires, confident that He will answer according to His will.

Our writing journey is about more than financial outcomes, it's a path of trust, purpose, and impact, where true provision and fulfillment come from following God's lead rather than chasing external measures of success. However, I must be honest, it can be challenging to secure funding for publishing, but remember that being called to write means you are also called to trust in God's timing and provision. There was a time when I received the greatest blessings in my writing journey simply when I let go of expecting immediate payment from others. Writing is not about the sale for me; it's about reaching the hearts of those who need to read my message. My first book only sold a handful of copies, but I found joy in the experience of writing. That journey inspired me to create a non-profit, impacting over 150,000 women in just three years! My writing led to further opportunities, including publishing, and even starting a successful business that thrived during challenging times, all because I placed my trust in God's provision rather than focusing solely on financial gain from that one book.

So, what am I saying? Stop measuring your worth as a writer by the lists of bestsellers, awards, or external validations. You are more than those rankings; you are a Kingdom Writer chosen to convey the love of Christ. If God desires your book to be on those lists, it will be. But our focus should truly be on fulfilling His purpose, not striving for fame. Trust in God's plan for your provision and success, and instead of worrying, concentrate on how you can please Him through your writing journey. With His guidance and provision, all things are possible, and you can have confidence that you are richly blessed.

GOD MEETS OUR NEEDS

God is the One who truly meets our needs. In Philippians 4:19, we learn that "God will supply all our needs according to His riches in glory." This means that even when we face tough times, we should remember that God is the ultimate provider. In our daily lives, it can be easy to worry about finances, friends, or rest, but God's promise assures us that He will take care of all these affairs. The Greek word for "supply" or "provision" is *epichorégia*. This means that God will give us the generous and sufficient help we need. So, we can trust Him, especially when we feel like we don't have what we need or when things are uncertain.

When we think about God meeting our needs, we can look to the story of Elijah as a powerful example. In 1 Kings 17:2-5, God instructs Elijah to go to a brook and drink water while He sends ravens to bring Elijah food. Can you imagine how difficult it must have been for Elijah? He could have easily felt anxious about following such odd instructions. However, Elijah chose to obey God, and in doing so, he found provision in the most unlikely ways. Just like Elijah, we might experience a sense of discomfort when God asks us to step out in faith. His instructions may seem challenging or unusual, but we can learn to trust Him, knowing that His ways are always for our good. As we embrace our uncomfortable obedience, it's important to remember that God delights in our prosperity. He wants us to thrive in our relationships, jobs, and every area of our lives. This includes big dreams and even the small joys of finding great deals at the store. God is not in the business of stealing, killing, or destroying our happiness; rather, He desires for us to have abundance. Remember, in Genesis 1:26, God commanded us to take dominion over the earth. This shows that He wants us to flourish and succeed, and that's something we can all hold on to in tough moments.

However, while we are encouraged to pursue our passions, including our calling to write, we must always keep our priorities straight. God has given us a beautiful commandment found in Deuteronomy 6:5: "You must love the Lord your God with all your heart, all your soul, and all your strength." This is a reminder that no matter how passionate we are about our dreams, including our desire to write, we can never place those dreams above our love for God. Our relationship with Him should always come first, guiding us as we fulfill our call in His name. We also should embrace the gifts we've been given without feeling jealous of others. Each person's talents are a testament to their obedience to God, and we must celebrate each unique contribution. When we learn to appreciate both our own gifts and those of others, it becomes easier to trust God's plan for our lives, even when we encounter seasons of uncertainty or challenge.

Let's not forget that trusting God to meet our needs is a journey of faith. Just like Elijah, we may face moments of uncertainty and discomfort, but those moments also serve as opportunities for us to grow closer to God. As we obey Him, we can rest assured that He will provide everything we need, whether it's a new job, relationships, or the strength to pursue our writing dreams. So, allow His love to fill your heart and let it inspire you as you navigate life. With God as our source, we can find peace, purpose, and fulfillment in all we do, knowing He is always there to provide.

THE POWER OF ANOINTING THROUGH WRITING

Have you ever wondered why the word "write" seems to echo in your mind, especially during life's toughest moments? This question puzzled me for a long time. It's as if writing becomes a guiding light when I face challenges. Whenever I pray or feel overwhelmed, that gentle prompt to write feels like an immediate answer to my struggles. It's interesting to note that while writing brings me comfort during dark days, it also calls to me in joyful moments. However, what stands out most is how I sensed this call even as a child. Whenever I faced disappointments and hardships, that same whisper to write would emerge. I often questioned whether God was truly listening or if I was simply imagining things. Little did I know, this urge to write was never random; it was connected to something much deeper.

Years later, I discovered the profound meaning behind this calling while preparing to be a part of and facilitate a transformative ministry known as Beauty for Ashes in Gainesville Georgia. This unique ministry allows individuals to express their feelings through drawing and writing when they are unable to use spoken words. Imagine being asked about your identity in Christ. Expressing this verbally can feel overwhelming or intimidating. But what if you were given paper and crayons to draw or write out your thoughts without any pressure? This creative outlet allows individuals to convey their feelings safely, at their own pace. It breaks down barriers and opens the door to healing because, sometimes, words can be too hard to find let alone speak. By using colors, shapes, and written words to express our innermost thoughts, we can begin to heal from past wounds. The beauty of this approach lies in its simplicity. When we use crayons, it reminds us of our childhood and the freedom that comes from uninhibited expression. There's no need to worry about judgment or the "right" way to communicate our stories. Instead, it's an opportunity to take a step forward, releasing what has been trapped inside. Often, those locked-away words can cause pain, and writing or drawing becomes the key to unlocking them. I've witnessed this transformation countless times in various support groups I've led. The moment I place a pack of crayons, pens, and paper in front of someone, their demeanor changes. Initially, they may look at me with confusion, wondering how drawing can possibly help and if I have lost my mind. However, as they begin to express themselves, the transformation is nothing short of miraculous! They become so absorbed in their drawings or writings that they lose track of time and their surroundings. It's as if the process of creating takes them beyond time and allows their hidden emotions to surface, paving the way for healing. This was made real for me through the teachings of the Bible. In Proverbs 18:21, we learn that "life and death are in the power of the tongue." Yet sometimes our hearts are too hurt to speak. Writing becomes an anointing, a divine tool for release, healing, and connection with our Creator. It helps us articulate what is difficult to express.

Many times, I've noticed that the same words we need to free ourselves from our pain are trapped deep within us. The act of writing or drawing with crayons is often a breakthrough moment for many. It's a simple yet powerful realization that the release of those revitalizing words can happen through this delightful medium. In fact, some of the most profound breakthroughs occur when someone finally opens up through their artwork. Just last week, a participant who had remained silent and withdrawn began sharing their story, which was beautifully captured in their drawings. It was a touching reminder of how God anoints our journeys, often in unexpected ways. This experience of writing and drawing serves as an incredible learning opportunity, not just for those who express themselves but for me as well. Each session reveals the undeniable power of storytelling, and how it can help us confront our pasts and embrace our identities in Christ. Throughout many sessions, participants have been able to connect their emotions to scripture, understanding how healing can occur when they allow God to guide their hands. This process fills my heart as I witness the transformation of individuals through the anointing of creativity.

I've found that writing is not just about expressing thoughts; it's also a tool for healing deeply rooted wounds. The gentle call to write is an invitation from God to explore the depths of our souls and release the burdens we carry. Just as King David wrote Psalms to pour out his heart, we too can find solace in our writing expressions.

It's a way of allowing God to flow through us, bringing healing and hope. So, when you feel that gentle nudge to write, embrace it. Discover the beauty of writing your story, for it is the anointing that breathes life into your journey!

A WRITER'S REVELATION ABOUT TIME

Time is a precious gift that often goes unnoticed until we experience a traumatic change in our lives. My mom always used to say that time is so precious and its worth more than money, a lesson I didn't truly grasp until a heartbreaking moment in my life. On July 8, 2023, everything changed when my mom went to bed and woke up in the presence of the Lord. That early morning call was like a thief in the night; it stole my joy and left me drowning in grief. I lost my guiding star, the person who had always been there for me, and suddenly I found myself facing the reality of how fragile life can be. As the Bible reminds us in Psalms 90:12, "Teach us to number our days, that we may gain a heart of wisdom." It was during this time of heartache that I finally began to understand the depth of my mother's words about time's importance.

The pain of losing my mother made me reflect deeply on the plans we had made together, dreams that now could never come true with her no longer being physically here with me. It struck me how suddenly her clock, the one that ticked for 67 years, had stopped without warning, and it was a shocking reminder that regardless of my plans, life has its expiration date. Sometimes, I think of her heart as a beautiful clock that had run its course, leaving behind memories, love, and lessons to cherish. The heartache then reminded me of those who say they don't have enough time to answer the call on their life or to do the things they love. It's easy to blame our busy lives, but I learned that it wasn't about a lack of time, it was how I was managing the time I had. In moments of grief, I started to see the truth: it's not just about making plans but prioritizing what truly matters.

After losing my mom, I realized that my life had taken a different turn. My days were filled with responsibilities that sometimes felt overwhelming. Yet, amid the grief, I was challenged to take a step back and consider how I used my time. The truth is, it wasn't just about feeling too busy; it was about being in control of my decisions and recognizing what I needed to change. Like Ecclesiastes 3:1 says, "To everything, there is a season, and a time for every matter under heaven." Perhaps the time had come for me to refocus on what I valued most, God, myself, my family, and my calling. In finding this clarity, I discovered an inspiring drive to make sure each moment counted, honoring my mother's legacy and her words of wisdom.

As I made these adjustments, I began to approach writing differently. I realized that the time I felt I lacked was actually several distractions disguised as busy days. Each day became a canvas, waiting for my thoughts to spill onto its pages. While it did require finding a rhythm in my schedule, I learned to delegate tasks and ask for help. Just as the Bible encourages us to bear one another's burdens (Galatians 6:2), I understood that sharing responsibilities could lead to more time for what truly mattered: creating to honor and glorify God, dreaming, loving, and cultivating current and new relationships with others. Writing became a joyful escape, a way for me to express my emotions and share my journey, reminding me that while life can be fleeting, our voices and stories can endure long after we're gone.

I have come to see time not simply as numbers ticking away but as an invaluable treasure that requires respect and careful handling. The depth of my sorrow transformed into a motivation to live fully, driven not by busyness but by intention. Each day holds the potential for growth, reflection, and connection. Through the love of my mother and the lessons I've learned, I understand now more than ever what it means to truly cherish our time.

So as Kingdom Writers, let's embrace the moments that make us laugh and cry, reminding ourselves that every tick of the clock is an invitation to love deeply, dream big, and live courageously. In everything we do, let's write and honor the time we have and the people we love, knowing that in the end, it's the relationships we build and the memories we create that will stay with us forever.

TESTIMONY OF EXPERIENCE

To be truthful, many of us, like myself, often find ourselves gazing into a mirror and whispering, "I'm not a writer. I just don't fit the mold." This mindset can be a significant hurdle. Reflecting on my childhood, writing was never presented as a path I could take. Instead, my future seemed set in stone, aimed toward business or medicine, as my parents were entrepreneurs and my grandmother was sure I would be a doctor. As for business, I started my training at the young age of eleven. I became familiar with the nuances of business by processing payroll and preparing bills for my parents' trucking company. My grandmother, a fierce woman with strong opinions, further reinforced this notion, boldly declaring that I had no choice but to become a doctor due to my less-than-stellar handwriting, which she called "chicken scratch." It's fascinating to think about how the words spoken over our lives can shape us, much like Proverbs 18:21 reminds us that the tongue has the power of life and death. Who knew one day I would earn my PhD and be an entrepreneur?

Despite the solid foundation laid by my family, there was an underlying calling to write that I couldn't quite grasp. I hadn't received any formal training. The only lessons I learned came from my grandmother's frustration when I handed in messy school assignments. I grew up with that feeling of inadequacy, which stuck with me through my teenage years. I still remember the times I spent sitting at the kitchen table, attempting to pen my thoughts, only to feel the weight of disapproval looming over me.

One pivotal moment was in Mrs. Windsor's English class during my senior year of high school. Her rigorous teaching style often left me overwhelmed and brought me to the brink of tears, as I constantly felt that nothing I produced was ever "good enough." While Mrs. Windsor shared my grandmother's sternness, I didn't recognize it at the time, what set her apart was that she saw potential in my writing that I couldn't yet see in myself.

The day my mother requested a meeting with Mrs. Windsor was a turning point in my life. In tears, I expressed my frustrations, feeling like my efforts were futile. But Mrs. Windsor, with her unwavering gaze and wise voice, looked straight at me and said, "I see something great in you." Those powerful words felt like a lifeline tossed to a drowning swimmer. I thought at first, she was just trying to appease me, especially with my mother forthrightly backing me up. Yet, in her declaration, I sensed that she truly believed in my potential, a belief I desperately needed. She encouraged me that, after completing her senior English class in high school, I would graduate from college without major issues if I simply focused and worked hard. And she was right, once I set my mind to something, obstacles faded as I began to succeed where I once thought I could not.

As I continued along my academic journey, I carried Mrs. Windsor's words with me. Nonetheless, insecurities resurfaced as I faced the ACT, where my struggles with writing became apparent once more. I did well in all areas except writing, leading to feelings of frustration and hopelessness, until a summer school English professor noticed my distress. After reading something I had written, she quickly assured me I didn't belong in remedial English, saying I wrote at a junior college level. She took the time to discuss my apprehensions about writing and helped me see that I had the ability to unleash my full potential. Although the fear persisted for a while, her faith in me put me into a new English class, ready to embrace the journey ahead.

Eventually, I discovered a surprising revelation in my forties, I came from a family of writers and creatives, although I hadn't recognized it before. These weren't just anybody; my grandmother wrote soulful poetry and heartfelt letters that moved the hearts of many. At family gatherings, her kind words were celebrated and seen almost as magical. My mother was also an incredible writer, known for her ministry, business, and technical writing, which inspired her community. When I look back at the things she wrote, I see how she created and wrote ideas that became real and came to life. She wrote and, as a result, created businesses, jobs for the community, ministries, charity work, and much more. My dad has a creative mind. Even though I didn't see him write a lot, I noticed how my mom and dad could take ideas, hammer them out, turn them into words, apply action, and become reality. They collaborated as a team, unaware that they were teaching their daughter how to tap into her God-given gift of creativity and express it through writing. The things they produced together were beyond imagination. Yet, during my childhood, I simply viewed them as my family, not as gifted writers and creatives. It took time for me to connect the dots and realize that writing was more than just a solitary pursuit, it was woven into the fabric of my family, reflecting God's creativity and love for me.

This new understanding encouraged me to explore my own calling more deeply. It wasn't until I met authors in person during a local seminar that I felt an even stronger connection to the world of writing. Meeting two authors, normal people with day-to-day challenges, rekindled my dreams. Our conversations shifted away from their books and took on a life of their own, filled with laughter and shared experiences. That interaction showed me that writers are indeed real, relatable individuals, and not some mythical creatures. I realized they share their stories for the blessing of others, just as I was compelled to share my own journey. It was in that moment, standing in line for a book signing, that I felt a flicker of inspiration urging me to embrace my calling as a writer and to honor the gift God had given me.

As I transitioned into the realm of writing, it became clear to me that every calling comes with sacrifices. To walk this path, I needed to dive deep into God's Word, allowing the Holy Spirit to guide my thoughts and expressions. I committed to studying and writing, often needing to pause social engagements and distractions to focus solely on this mission. This might not be the case for everyone, but I felt an intense urge to do what God wanted me to do. I learned that obedience often requires patience and understanding with a heart full of trust, just as we're reminded in Proverbs 3:5-6. The journey, while daunting, led me to appreciate the subtle beauty of growth, no matter how slow or painful it was. It taught me that as I write, my conversations with God become a crucial aspect of my work.

Now, each piece I write is born not just from my experiences, but from a heart willing to trust in the Lord. I ask myself important questions along the way: Does my writing align with God's Word? Does it glorify Him? Am I authentically sharing my testimony? Each question serves as a compass, guiding my efforts toward fulfilling my divine calling. In doing so, I've come to realize that my journey may have twists and turns, but they are all part of a greater plan. God intricately weaves our life stories into His magnificent tapestry, and as I continue to write, I embrace the belief that my words can bring hope, healing, and inspiration to others, just as I received from those who poured into me. With each line that flows through my fingertips, I feel the unconditional love of God affirming my place in this world, reminding me to keep writing and to never lose hope.

FINANCIAL PROVISION FOR WRITERS

As I talk to current and aspiring writers, a common question arises: What should one do when life gets tough? Especially when finances are tight, many people find themselves struggling. In the Bible, Hebrews 11:1 tells us that "faith shows the reality of what we hope for; it is the evidence of things we cannot see." This truth resonates deeply in the world of writing and publishing. I have had the privilege of experiencing both sides, not only as a writer who dreams of getting published but also as a publisher who helps others achieve their dreams. Over the years, I've asked countless writing colleagues why they hesitate to write and publish, and I've routinely received three main answers: a lack of time, money, and experience. Interestingly, when I switched roles and interviewed them as a publisher, the responses remained the same.

However, through my journey, I discovered that provision extends beyond these three resources, especially for those facing financial obstacles. I encountered several writers who, despite their struggles, felt called to write and, through their obedience, God provided for them. It was as if doors that once seemed closed suddenly swung wide open, allowing these writers opportunities they never imagined possible. One such instance was during my time in a dream builder group. My passion was to publish testimonies for writers, and there I crossed paths with a remarkable woman eager to share her own story. At the end of a session, she boldly approached me, expressing her desire for me to publish her testimony. Despite her lack of funds, she exuded faith, declaring, "I trust God."

That night, I took her words to heart, asking the Lord if I could give her a scholarship and figure out how to pay her publishing fees myself. Yet, God had a different plan for me. He instructed me to charge her just as I did with others, leading me to focus on her story rather than the financial aspects.

Nervously, I shared the necessary amount with her, fully aware of how essential her testimony was to be heard. To my astonishment, she responded with unwavering faith, proclaiming that God would provide for her. In our shared moment outside, we prayed together, entrusting her journey into God's hands. Shortly thereafter, I received a call from someone expressing a desire to cover her book's publishing fees but asked to remain anonymous. This was just one of many instances where generous strangers stepped in to support authors facing financial challenges in bringing their work to publication.

I noticed a consistent pattern in these situations: the writers began to write before any financial support materialized. They displayed remarkable confidence and creativity, regardless of their current monetary status. It was almost as if their faith activated an atmosphere of provision around them. Writing while trusting God positions you for incredible blessings. As Kingdom Writers, we are privy to an essential truth, articulated in Philippians 4:19: "My God will supply all my needs." These writers pressed on with their work, even when faced with life's financial hurdles, refusing to let their manuscripts gather dust in drawers. Instead, they stayed active, speaking their stories into existence and inspiring me with their unwavering dedication.

Reflecting on my own experiences, I realize that many people, much like my past self, become overly focused on their financial burdens, which can halt their creative flow. I remember when I was a single mother working endless hours just to make ends meet. I felt exhausted but realized that writing was my lifeline. Early mornings became my new best friend as I carved out just fifteen to thirty minutes to put pen to paper. Slowly, my story took shape, and soon, I found myself stepping into opportunities I never thought possible. My writing journey blossomed into a nonprofit organization, and we eventually expanded our reach internationally. Through my persistence to trust God and His guidance, I exited the grueling work routine that once consumed my life.

The lesson here is profound. Often, the breakthroughs we seek in our personal lives are intricately linked to our obedience in writing. As you compose your own stories, speak courageously about your desires. Claim your financial abundance as you declare, "Bank account, fill up! Bills, be paid!" Remember that God has given writers like you and me the authority to use our words powerfully. Just like a skilled archer aiming at a target, we can direct our prayers and intentions with clarity and purpose. Embrace your creativity, trust in God's provision, and let your writing pave the way for your dreams. Your journey may not always be easy, but with faith and perseverance, you can witness incredible transformation.

PERSONAL PROVISION

When we think about personal provision, it's important to recognize how God meets the desires of our hearts, especially for those of us who have a call on our life to write. Time and time again, I have witnessed firsthand the miraculous ways God delivers not only financial provision but also emotional and spiritual blessings to writers who are obedient and take steps of faith. For instance, I've had the joy of watching many talented writers from our publishing company find incredible spouses. Some might chalk this up to mere coincidence, but how do you explain that every writer we supported who longed for a spouse has now entered into marriage? Also, not just any kind of marriage, but marriages that are healthy, thriving, and God-honoring. God works in wonderous and mysterious ways, and these moments emphasize the power of faith and the supportive community that surrounds us. Moreover, the stories don't stop at relationships; they extend into exciting opportunities, such as when a writer expressed her dream to speak in a foreign country and soon found herself sharing her message on a platform in Africa.

It's fascinating to consider how these experiences illustrate that God's provision transcends financial support. Truly, many remarkable stories shine a light on healing and miracles that come through the written word. The ones that warm my heart are when a writer shares about someone they thought would never choose to follow Christ, only to discover that their words inspired that very person to embrace their faith. This is the essence of personal provision, it's about fulfilling deep desires, nudging us toward healing, and blessing others through our talents. As we explore the depths of provision, we need to grasp that it encompasses all aspects of our lives, not just the financial realm.

Now, by understanding this greater picture, it's essential to remember that our role as writers comes with a responsibility. We must boldly ask in Jesus' name for what we need, and trust that He will provide it. Philippians 2:9-11 tells us that Jesus' name is above every name, meaning His power extends beyond our material concerns to help us overcome our insecurities as writers. This is not meant to be taken lightly; our prayers should align not with mere wishes, but with heartfelt intentions. When we pray, we tap into the Spirit and ask for guidance that reflects our commitment to use our voices not solely for personal gain but to uplift others.

When insecurity creeps in, it can be overwhelming, but we can find comfort in bringing those worries to God. By asking in Jesus' name, we can transform our writing into a vessel of blessing for others. If you desire to catch God's attention, seek resources that enable you to help those around you. In our creative journeys, we can request the tools we need to improve, along with the wisdom to apply them effectively. It's in these moments of earnest prayer and intention that we can truly make a difference, both in our lives and in the lives of our readers.

Remember, seeking God's provision through writing isn't just about achieving personal success. It's about creating a ripple effect of love, encouragement, and inspiration. With every word penned, there lies an opportunity for renewal, healing, and connection. That's why we must remain open, trust the process, and ask for divine assistance in our writing ventures. In doing so, we join a legacy of Kingdom Writers whose prayers are rooted in purpose and who understand the profound impact of words. As we embark on this journey, may we always strive to honor God and be instruments of His grace, reminding ourselves and others of the incredible gifts He has in store for those who dare to believe.

CHAPTER 2 SUMMARY: TRUSTING GOD IN OUR WRITING JOURNEY

In this chapter, we learn that writing is not just a personal journey, but a way to share God's light with others. As writers in God's Kingdom, we need to remember that God will provide for our needs if we only have faith. The Bible teaches us to believe in God's promises, and we should celebrate our unique talents rather than comparing ourselves to others. Writing is a gift from God, and it can help us connect with Him and others when we express our needs and desires.

We find hope in Philippians 4:13, reminding us that we can do everything through Christ who strengthens us, even when we feel unsure. As we write, we must trust God's plan, knowing our efforts can lead to blessings for both others and ourselves. By sharing our personal stories and acts of kindness, we can open doors to new opportunities and blessings.

The chapter also emphasizes how important it is to have faith, especially when we face financial difficulties or challenges. Just like Elijah who received food from ravens, we are reminded that God often meets our needs in unexpected ways. We should look to God for support, prioritizing our love for Him above our dreams while pursuing those dreams with passion.

Lastly, we are encouraged to see writing as a potential source of healing, both for ourselves and others. God can use our writing to bring nourishment to our souls and the hearts of others.

ACTION STEPS

1. **Pray for Guidance:** Start each writing session by asking God to guide your thoughts and words. Think about what you want to express and how it can help others.
2. **Trust God:** Remind yourself daily that God provides everything you need. When you feel anxious about your writing or finances, read Philippians 4:19, which assures us that God will supply our needs.
3. **Celebrate Your Gifts:** Make a list of your writing talents and unique abilities. Share them with others in your community to encourage and uplift one another.
4. **Share Your Stories:** Write about your experiences, challenges, and faith. Understand that your story can inspire others and help them in their journeys.
5. **Ask for Help**: Just as God provided for Elijah in unexpected ways, be open to seeking assistance from friends or local resources when faced with obstacles in your writing journey.
6. **Practice Gratitude:** Take time each day to thank God for His blessings and for the opportunity to write. Write down things you are grateful for to remind yourself of His goodness.

By following these action steps, you can deepen your relationship with God through writing and trust in His perfect timing.

CHAPTER 3
Life Challenges

LIFE CHALLENGES

WHEN WE ARE NOT FOCUSED on issues of provision, we often face life challenges that hinder our writing. Life is full of challenges, and how we respond to them can shape who we are. As we embark on our journey in life, especially those of us called to be Kingdom Writers, we may face opposition and hardships, and even great loss, but these tough times help cultivate an inner strength that is often used for our next season. Remember the story of David, who was anointed to be king but faced many trials before he took the throne. It's important to understand that our struggles can prepare us for what lies ahead, so we should not rush through them, but instead seek God's guidance through prayer and ask Him what we can learn amidst our hardships.

In life, we will all face trials, whether we are followers of Christ or not, because we live in a fallen world. The Bible tells us in 1 Peter 1:7 that our faith is tested through trials, much like gold is refined in fire. These challenges help us build a genuine faith that ultimately brings glory to God. Our stories and testimonies become richer when we endure hardships. If you are feeling like you're falling behind in fulfilling your calling as a writer, remember that God's timing is perfect. If you feel like it's too late to write your book because of the hard times you've faced, don't think that way! The only time it's truly too late to write your book is when you're no longer alive. So, keep in mind that many people need to read what you have to say and remember, God can redeem the time. As it says in Joel 2:25, "I will restore to you the years that the swarming locust has eaten."

It's essential to recognize that life challenges do not stop the mission God has placed in your heart. Think about the stories of Daniel in the lion's den and the three Hebrew boys who faced the fiery furnace. Their faith and unwavering trust in God saved them despite their dire circumstances.

Remember, our response to life's challenges should stem from our beliefs rather than our fears. Fear can paralyze us and make us feel as though we do not have what it takes to overcome obstacles. Instead of succumbing to that fear, let's cling to faith, our source of strength, knowing that God equips us to handle what we face.

As we navigate life as Kingdom Writers, it's crucial to stay grounded in the Word of God. James 1:5 encourages us to seek wisdom from God, finding reassurance in knowing that He will provide guidance to those who ask. Surround your writing journey in prayer and Scripture; this is where we build our foundation. The Lord instructs us to be wise like a person who builds their house on solid rock (Matthew 7:24). By immersing ourselves in His Word while tackling our daily challenges, we are better equipped to respond to issues with faith and strength.

We must understand that Scripture is our sword in battle; we must know how to wield it to fight against distractions, discouragement, and doubt. Life will throw us curveballs, but these moments can often become our greatest testimonies. Just like Timothy faced external persecution as well as internal struggles, the path to fulfilling our calling may not always be easy. However, Paul encouraged him to stir up the gifts God had placed within him (2 Timothy 1:6). As Kingdom Writers, we must remember to share our unique messages through our written words, regardless of the challenges. It may seem easier to shrink back during tough times, but our call is to speak boldly. God has placed gifts in each of us; all we must do is fan those flames and use our voices to spread His truth.

Additionally, it's important not to let life's distractions diminish our joy or drive for writing. The enemy seeks to bombard us with distractions, making us feel we are not capable or equipped to fulfill our purpose. Can I tell you a secret? A problem is just another opportunity to develop your character. The essence behind problems is the issue of distractions. Distractions keep you from living the life promised to you. When faced with overwhelming problems, distractions, and trials, let's hold on to the truth that God is working behind the scenes, even when we can't see it. Our struggles are not wasted; they become the foundation upon which God can build a message that can touch many lives. Just like Joseph, who rose to prominence after years of adversity, we too will one day realize the purpose behind our trials.

Each challenge we face can lead us closer to God and refine our writing journeys. Let us decide to respond not from fear, but with faith, tapping into the instruction provided in His Word. We may look at our circumstances and see only obstacles, but God sees potential. Remember, every moment of difficulty can be coupled with divine intervention. Amidst our struggles, God is creating a beautiful story of hope and redemption. As we trust Him in the valleys and celebrate victories on the mountaintops, let's remember that we are never alone. Our testimonies serve not only as proof of God's faithfulness, but as powerful words of encouragement for others. We are called to inspire through our pen, and every trial is part of that beautiful journey.

SELF-DOUBT

Self-doubt is a huge life challenge that many of us face, and I must admit, it's something I have struggled with too. Even while writing this collection, I found some of those insecurities creeping back in. For many years after I published my books, I didn't feel qualified to label myself as a writer. One particular moment stands out, when I was at a local gym, taking a water aerobics class. I had been attending this class for about a month when some of the ladies and I started chatting. One of them asked what I did for a living. I confidently listed all my jobs and accomplishments, and at the end, I quickly and softly mentioned that I had written some books. One of the ladies loudly said, "Wow, you're a writer," and I instantly felt uncomfortable. My mind buzzed with questions: Am I a real writer? Is just writing enough to make me one? Why did I even say anything about writing?

I wish I had an official degree in writing or some shiny awards to prove my talent, but I didn't. I wasn't even a full-time writer, nor did I have a job title that included the word "writer" in it. Heck, I wrote my last book seven years ago. So instead, I told myself that I was an entrepreneur or a leader who simply wrote a few books back in the day. When I shared my feelings with the lady who had commented on my being a writer, I felt a heaviness in my heart as I declared, "I'm not a writer." After saying those words, it felt like I had lost something precious. It was as if a part of my spirit was saying, "You've denied the gift I have given you." My new water aerobics friend looked puzzled, which only fueled my insecurities further. She asked me, "What makes a writer if it isn't writing, publishing books, and also teaching and publishing others?" In that moment, I was left speechless, like a deer caught in headlights. The doubts that filled my mind made it hard to respond. I had spent years believing that I wasn't cut out to be a writer because I didn't fit some nonsense doubt that had planted itself in my mind and taken root.

As I reflected on my past, I felt overwhelmed with thoughts of my personal struggles and responsibilities for others. The idea of dedicating time to developing my writing skills felt impossible, and I convinced myself that real writers lived lives I could never relate to, understand, or imagine. Yet, deep down, I felt God calling me to write. It was uncomfortable to think that maybe I had missed something important. After that conversation, a quiet voice nestled in my heart whispered, "You were a writer before you wrote your first word." I was completely taken aback. That simple statement shook me to my core. How could I be a writer before I had even written anything?

When I think about Esther's story, I see how important timing is. Sometimes in life, everything comes together just right, just like it did for Esther. She was a girl without parents who ended up in the king's palace at just the right moment. God had a plan for her to help her people during a big crisis. In Esther 4:14, it says, "If you keep quiet at a time like this, deliverance and relief for the Jews will arise from some other place, but you and your relatives will die. Who knows if perhaps you were made queen for just such a time as this?" Esther showed us that being faithful and trusting in God is powerful, even if it's tough. This connects with Romans 8:28, which tells us that God makes everything work out for good for those who love Him. Esther's story teaches us that our call might not be easy, but we must trust that God has us in the right place at the right time for a special reason.

Unfortunately, we, unlike Esther, often overlook our potential because of the insecurities that cloud our vision. Instead of stepping forward in faith, we let fear hold us back. Just like Esther, we should remember that our worth doesn't come from our titles or experiences. God sees us for who we are created to be, not just by what we have done or achieved. It's essential to recognize that self-doubt can keep us from living out our true callings. When we focus on our insecurities rather than God's promises, we miss out on the incredible adventures He has prepared for us.

In Isaiah 12:2, we learn that "God has come to save me. I will trust in him and not be afraid. The Lord God is my strength and my song; he has given me victory." This verse beautifully captures the essence of overcoming our insecurities. We are never expected to navigate our journeys alone; we have God, who empowers us to rise above our fears and doubts. He has provided us all with victory.

I encourage each of you to examine the negative thoughts and insecurities that hold you back. Every person has a unique gift to offer the world. Embrace the truth that you are worthy and remember that God has a purpose for you. Writing and sharing your story can inspire, heal, and uplift others. Let go of the idea that you're unqualified and hold on tightly to the truth: you are called and equipped just as you are. With each step forward, allow yourself to celebrate progress, however small. Remember, you are more capable than you realize, and your voice matters.

FALSE IDENTITY

Have you ever thought about how our personalities shape our talents? Sometimes, we believe that certain traits define what we can or cannot do. For instance, many writers are seen as introverts, people who find their energy and inspiration from within. This idea is commonly embraced, and when you look online, you'll often find titles like "Why Introverts Make the Best Writers." However, being more of an extrovert doesn't mean you lack writing talent or that you can't tap into the creative spirit that God has given you. Extroverts often find inspiration from the world around them, engaging with other people and experiences to spark their creativity. This is not a reason to doubt your abilities; it just shows that everyone has a different way of expressing their gifts.

Reflecting on my journey, I realize that I once let this belief control my thoughts about myself. I thought that because I'm an ambivert (introvert and extrovert), I could never be a true or good writer. This belief was both misleading and damaging, creating a false identity that limited my creative potential. Instead of viewing my strength as an ambivert, which lets me adapt to my setting and audience, I let doubt creep in, making me think I couldn't create meaningful art with my words. I was basically neutral and concluded it was best for me to just sit on the fence and look over at the extroverts and introverts and be satisfied with watching them. The Bible teaches us to take our thoughts captive (2 Corinthians 10:5), a valuable lesson that reminds us to challenge which thoughts we allow to define us. I wish I had recognized sooner that my ambivert nature is a gift to the world of writing. I have a unique ability to relate to and reach introverts *and* extroverts. Definitely something the enemy did not want me to know.

As we explore our identities and the labels, we place on ourselves, it's important to remember that our true identity comes from God, not our traits. Each of us is uniquely designed with different strengths and weaknesses, and that includes how we express our creativity when writing. I've learned that God has a special plan for all of us, whether we are introverts, extroverts, or ambiverts. When we align our understanding of who we are with God's perspective, we discover that

He sees us as beloved creations capable of amazing things. So, let's embrace our uniqueness, knowing that we are equipped to fulfill our calling through Christ. When you think about it, we all have stories to tell, and our experiences shape those narratives. An extrovert might bring the vibrant energy of human connection to their writing, while an introvert might explore the depths of solitude and reflection. Both perspectives are essential and serve a purpose in the grand picture of storytelling. Embracing who we are allows us to bring authenticity to our writing, making it more relatable to others. It's not about fitting into a specific mold but rather honoring the individuality that God created us with.

So, let's cast off the chains of false identities and step into the light of who we truly are. Celebrate your unique approach to writing and know that your voice matters, regardless of your personality type. Remember, God's purpose can shine through you in incredible ways, bringing inspiration and hope to those who read your words. Allow your creativity to flow freely, just as God intended, and watch as He transforms not only your journey but also the hearts of many who encounter your work. Together, we can encourage one another to embrace our true selves and share the gifts we've been blessed with, creating a brighter world through our stories.

FEAR OF NOT BEING ENOUGH

The fear of not being enough is something many of us struggle with, and it's a heavy burden to carry. Imagine standing at the threshold of your dreams, filled with hopes and aspirations, yet feeling paralyzed by doubts and fears. A wise professor once shared an important lesson with me about this feeling. He pointed out that when we speak using the word "but," we often connect two opposing ideas, creating a conflict within ourselves. For instance, we might say, "I want to write a book, but I am not a writer." This simple declaration can halt our progress and stifle our creativity. Instead of seeing possibilities, we end up overwhelmed by our insecurities, allowing the flood gates of fear and doubt to open in our lives. It's as if we let our fears drown out our hopes, whispering doubts that we will never be enough.

The moment I became aware of this habit, it was like waking up from a deep sleep. The Holy Spirit began to gently correct my language and my mindset. Each time I said, "I want to do this, but…" I felt an uncomfortable tug in my heart. This tug was a reminder that I was limiting myself with my own words. God encourages us not to dwell in fear, but to trust in His strength. The Bible tells us, "I can do all things through Christ who strengthens me" (Philippians 4:13). This verse was a lifeline for me. It reminded me that I am capable of achieving my dreams, not because of my own strength, but through God's support. When we lean into encouragement from God, we can push past the "buts" that hold us back.

Thinking about how I can become a writer inspired me to replace those limiting phrases with affirmations. Instead of saying, "I want to write a book, but I am not a writer," I began proclaiming, "I am on the journey to becoming the writer God created me to be!" This simple shift allowed me to open my heart to possibilities instead of being closed off. Transformation began as I viewed writing not as a daunting task, but as an adventure. I learned to appreciate each small step I took toward my goal. It is in these small steps that we often find our strength. In fact, even the Bible encourages us in this way in Zechariah 4:10: "Do not despise these small beginnings, for the Lord rejoices to see the work begin."

As I struggled with feelings of inadequacy, I began to understand more deeply that these fears often mask our true potential. We can learn to embrace who we are and believe in the gifts that have been bestowed upon us. Each one of us is intricately designed by our Creator, which means we all have a unique purpose. When we allow fear to cloud our vision, we forget about the incredible things we are capable of achieving. The journey may not always be easy, but it is one worth embarking on. With faith as our foundation, we can step boldly into our futures, discarding our worries and fears and replacing them with hope and resilience.

Banishing the fear of not being enough starts by changing the way we think and speak. I'll go into greater detail in the following chapter, but for now, know this: With the help of the Holy Spirit, and the reassurance from God's word, we can replace "buts" with affirmations that empower us. When we acknowledge our fears and invite God into them, we can conquer the obstacles that block our paths. Always remember that you are enough just as you are. Every time doubts arise, turn to the Word of God for encouragement. Let His promises lift you up and remind you that through Him, all things are possible. So let go of those fears, embrace your dreams, and step into the person you were created to be!

HAVING MANY GIFTS AND TALENTS IS A BLESSING, NOT A CURSE.

The gift of writing is truly amazing, right? But have you ever wondered why some writers seem to have many other talents too? And why do they keep finding new gifts they didn't even know they had? I want to share with you some lessons I learned from an event I attended a few years ago. It was very interesting and eye-opening. At this conference, many people talked about their different gifts and talents. We were informed that each of us has special abilities connected to our purpose in life. Many creative people at this event shared that they often felt overwhelmed by all the gifts they possessed. Instead of using these talents to inspire others, some turned to social media for advice, or even paid people to help them, which sometimes led to them using their gifts in ways that didn't feel right. Others felt confused and frustrated. But in our search for answers, we all, including myself, missed something important: God has bigger plans for us than just following others' advice, scrolling through social media, or even making money. I don't want you to get me wrong, I believe that our gifts can help us with the provision we need. My mom used to say, "All you have is all you need; God will provide the rest," and I truly believe that. However, our talents are not just for making money. They should be used to help others, to encourage them, and to guide them toward Christ. When we focus only on getting rich, we might forget the real purpose of our abilities. Instead of asking others how to use our gifts, we should be asking God how *He* wants us to use what He has given us. James 1:5 tells us that if we ask God for wisdom, He will give it to us.

Many writers struggle to comprehend their multiple gifts and talents. They constantly learn, grow, and master new skills, yet they wonder why they are so versatile. Why not just one focused gift, like a professional vocalist or a world-renowned artist? I, too, struggled with this personally, so this question lingered in my heart for months after that conference, leading me to prayerful reflections. Then one day, the Holy Spirit gently reminded me that this diversity in my talents and gifts is a blessing, particularly in writing. It allows me to connect with various audiences. Rather than viewing it as a burden, it's important to recognize that having multiple gifts can draw in a wider audience and open doors to share Christ with more people.

As writers with divine gifts, we must embrace our versatility. Each talent we possess can complement our writing and enhance our reach. The more people we connect with, the greater opportunity to lead them to Christ. This is a powerful truth that the enemy desperately wants to keep us blinded to. When we approach our writing as a calling rather than merely a big payday, we understand how our abilities can serve a higher purpose. In using our varied talents to share messages of hope and love, we are fulfilling our role as Kingdom Writers. Remember, the enemy wishes to distract us from recognizing the incredible potential we have in writing. Each word we put on paper can resonate deeply and transform lives. So let us not measure our gifts based on finances, but by the impact they can have. By allowing God to direct our paths, we can use our writing to touch hearts and lead nations to Christ. Embrace your gifts, nurture them, and let them shine through your words. They are much more than mere talents; they are powerful tools designed to change the world.

———

CHAPTER 3 SUMMARY: OVERCOMING LIFE'S CHALLENGES AND EMBRACING OUR CALLING

Life is full of challenges, and how we react to them shapes who we are. No matter how tough things get, God sees our struggles. He has already paid the price for us through Jesus. As Kingdom Writers, we will face difficult situations or circumstances, but these experiences help us grow stronger for what's ahead. Just like David, who had to overcome many trials before becoming king, our struggles prepare us for our future. It is also important to understand that, even as righteous people, we will face suffering, struggles, and challenges because we live in a fallen world. As it says in John 16:33, "In this world, you will have trouble. But take heart! I have overcome the world."

Once we give our lives to Christ, we are justified. I will talk more about justification in chapter six of this book. For now, I just want you to understand that justification happens right after you have given your life to Christ. When you sincerely say the prayer for salvation and end with "Amen," God views you as righteous. Your identity forever changes, and no one can take that away from you. It's important to know that there is nothing you can do to earn this. Along with this gift, there are three benefits of justification that I would like to share with you. The first benefit is being at peace with God. Secondly, you gain access to God. Third, you receive the hope of God's glory, which brings joy from the coming King and assures us that we have a bright future ahead. Therefore, when a justified person (someone who has given their life to Christ through the prayer of salvation) understands these truths, they will have a mindset that no challenge in life can defeat them. They have peace, access to God, and hope, which will strengthen their character in Christ. As Romans 5:1-2 tells us, "Therefore, since we have been justified through faith, we have peace with God through our Lord Jesus Christ."

It's important to pray and seek God's wisdom during hard times. The Bible tells us in 1 Peter 1:7 that our faith is tested like gold being refined in fire. The hard times we face can build our faith and bring glory to God. Even if you feel behind in your writing journey, remember that it's never too late. God can make up for lost time, just as He did for many in the Bible. Life's challenges won't stop God's mission. Think about Daniel in the lion's den, or the three friends in the fiery furnace. Their faith saved them in tough times. Instead of responding out of fear, we must cling to our faith as they did. James 1:5 tells us to ask God for wisdom! He will guide us. As writers, it's vital to surround ourselves with prayer and God's Word. Remember the story of the wise man who built his house on the rock (Matthew 7:24). By relying on Scripture, we can tackle our challenges with confidence and strength.

ACTION STEPS

1. **Pray for Guidance:** Take time to ask God what you can learn from your struggles.
2. **Read the Bible Regularly:** Immerse yourself in God's Word to build a strong foundation for your writing.
3. **Seek Community Support:** Find other writers or friends who can pray with you and offer encouragement.
4. **Embrace Your Journey:** Accept that your unique story, including the difficult parts, contributes to your writing.
5. **Replace Negative Thoughts:** When doubt creeps in, counter it with affirmations from Scripture, like Philippians 4:13.
6. **Stay Focused on Your Calling:** Remember that your writing has the power to inspire and uplift others.

God sees the potential in us, even when things are tough. Each experience can help us grow closer to Him and refine our gifts as writers. Let's trust God through the good and tough times, knowing He is with us every step of the way.

CHAPTER 4
Mental Health

THOUGHT LIFE

DID YOU KNOW that you are the CEO of your thoughts? It's true! Think of your mind as the company that you lead. Every day, you make decisions about what to think and believe. Just like a CEO manages their business, you manage your mind. One crucial responsibility you have is to take hold of negative thoughts and bring them under control. The Bible tells us in 2 Corinthians 10:5 that we should "take every thought captive to obey Christ." This means you can choose to either feed those negative thoughts or starve them. As a Kingdom Writer, this skill is incredibly powerful in helping you walk confidently in the purpose God has for you. Remember, the enemy may try to disrupt your thoughts, but he cannot read your mind. So, when thoughts of doubt arise that make you feel unqualified to write, simply turn them around and declare, "I am a Kingdom Writer. I am qualified to write what God reveals to me."

It's important for writers, current and aspiring, to understand that there are forces that want to distort how we view ourselves and our work. Much like the story of Eve in the garden, where a mix of truth and lies tempted her, we face similar challenges. The enemy told Eve that she would surely not die if she ate the apple, but even though she didn't drop dead right away, she faced spiritual death, and later, physical death with all of humanity. This teaches us that the enemy often lies, no matter how cleverly the lies are presented. When we start believing these falsehoods, our self-image and how we think God sees us can change for the worse. It's crucial to remember Hebrews 13:8, which tells us, "Jesus Christ is the same yesterday, today, and forever." This verse assures us that God's miracles and truths from the past still ring true in our lives today. Clinging to God's truth can act as a guiding light, driving away the darkness of doubt, lies, and fear.

When I first started my writing journey, it was hard for me to believe that I was a writer. Even when others praised my work, I would smile and nod, but inside, I felt unworthy of that title. I found it much easier to encourage others to write, while I often doubted my own abilities. Thoughts in my mind whispered that I could never be good enough at anything, especially writing. Instead of taking charge as the CEO of my own thoughts, I acted like a temporary employee nervously hoping that no one would see me working. This mindset made everything harder, filling my heart with insecurities that turned into excuses that held me back. I would tell myself that I wasn't educated enough or experienced enough, that I didn't have enough book sales, and that I had no writing awards to validate my writing. This fear shaped my attitude, making it hard for me to share my heart or express my thoughts with others. Breaking free from this cycle felt impossible, and it seemed like my entire world relied on the lies those negative thoughts told me. But I remembered Isaiah 41:10: "Don't be afraid, for I am with you. Don't be discouraged, for I am your God. I will strengthen you and help you. I will hold you up with my victorious right hand." With faith, I began to see that accepting myself as a writer was not just a fearful dream, but my calling and I was determined to make it a reality.

In my journey as a writer, I discovered a turning point during a critical thinking class in Bible college. It was there that God started to bring light into my darkness. Through my professor, I learned valuable lessons and found His truth, which encouraged me to embrace my calling as a writer, even when doubts and insecurities arose. Having moved to a new state where I no one, I realized that I had tied my identity to people, my past achievements, and experiences. I never viewed myself as anything more than what others determined I could achieve or accomplish, especially when it came to being a writer. Reflecting on this, I realized that the fear of not measuring up is a common struggle for many writers, but God's truth empowers us to move beyond those limitations and step confidently into our calling.

In the world of writing, it's common to feel unqualified, which can lead to a limited mindset. For me, I often found comfort in writing short snippets, like brief devotionals and challenges. These little pieces felt safer to me than jumping into the deeper waters of writing longer works. I was afraid of the judgment I might face from sharing bigger pieces that exposed my thoughts and feelings completely. However, the Bible reminds us in 2 Timothy 1:7, "For God has not given us a spirit of fear, but of power and of love and of a sound mind." This teaches us that we should not let our fears hold us back. Instead, we can embrace our gifts and share them boldly, knowing that we are supported and loved by God.

After recognizing that I did not need to fear, God gently nudged me toward growth. He encouraged me while living in a new place where we knew no one, to see myself as He does in front of a new, much more diverse audience. Every time someone asked, "What do you do for a living?" my heart would race with anxiety. This was my moment to confront those insecurities and remember what God says about me. As it says in Romans 8:16, "For his Spirit joins with our spirit to affirm that we are God's children." I am a child of God, redeemed by the blood of Jesus. Through His redemption, I reclaimed my heritage and found justification, knowing that I was redeemed, justified, forgiven, and chosen. Therefore, I proudly embraced my truth: "I am a Kingdom Writer." This affirmation not only lifted my spirits, but it solidified my understanding of my purpose in this calling.

I must be honest, it wasn't easy, especially at first. I thought I would feel more confident right away, but it turned out to be a gradual process. To introduce myself as a writer, I learned that I needed to take control of my negative thoughts. The first step was realizing that I had power over my own mind. Just as a good CEO manages a company, I had the responsibility to manage my thoughts and not let them lead me in the wrong direction. I had to ask myself how I treated these bad thoughts. Were they trapped away in a dark dungeon, ignored and forgotten? Or was I caring for them like a family member who needed a place to stay? I realized that I needed to feed my thoughts with positive truths from God's Word instead of allowing them to thrive on lies and insecurities. By creating a nurturing environment for my mind, I began to feel more confident and reflect on the truth of who God says I am. Let me be honest with you, even now, as I write this book, I still have negative thoughts that try to creep in. But as I continue writing my story, I thank God for this journey. I trust that He will shape my thoughts and guide my writing, helping me to focus on glorifying Him rather than my doubts. I also learned that my identity is rooted in Him, not just in the calling to write. As Romans 12:2 reminds us, "Don't copy the behavior and customs of this world, but let God transform you into a new person by changing the way you think. Then you will learn to know God's will for you, which is good and pleasing and perfect." Embracing this truth can lead us all to a healthier thought life, especially as writers. Recognizing this ongoing battle with our thoughts, it becomes essential for us as writers to intentionally ground ourselves in God's truth, especially when doubts and insecurities threaten to hold us back.

As writers, we often come face-to-face with challenges that test our confidence and our thought processes. When these moments arise, it's vital to ask yourself, "What is my 'it is written'?" This means we need to examine our thoughts and see how they align with the Bible. For example, you may sometimes feel unworthy when it comes to writing, thinking, "I can't be a writer because I lack talent or support." During such times, remind yourself of Philippians 4:19, which tells us, "And this same God who takes care of me will supply all your needs from his glorious riches, which have been given to us in Christ Jesus." This reflects the heart of our journey as writers. We must cling to God's Word to combat the doubts that threaten our creativity.

Take a moment to think about a negative thought that holds you back. Write it down on paper. Next, find a scripture that speaks truth to that thought. Our minds can filter out a lot of information, but it is crucial to consider what we use for our filter. For instance, if someone says, "You won't succeed as a writer," we can respond with God's reassurance from Jeremiah 1:5, "I knew you before I formed you in your mother's womb. Before you were born I set you apart and appointed you as my prophet to the nations." This reminds us that God has a plan for us and has given us a purpose. When we let other people's opinions overpower what God says about us, we weaken our mental strength and defenses. To fight against this negativity, we need to surround ourselves with God's Word, allowing it to fortify our minds and help us stand strong as writers. By intentionally filtering our thoughts through the truth of God's Word, we can guard our minds against negativity and stand firm in our calling, even when doubts try to creep in.

As Kingdom Writers, it's important to be watchful and not let negativity take hold of our thoughts. The enemy is eager to sow seeds of doubt. We must remember that while the devil can introduce harmful thoughts into our minds, we have the power to choose whether we accept or reject them. Many writers struggle with thoughts like "I am not a writer" or "I will never be successful." Instead of giving in to these lies, let's replace them with uplifting truths: "I am a writer, chosen by God to share His message with others." With this awareness, it becomes even more important to actively guard our minds, recognizing the difference between the enemy's lies and God's truth so we can stay focused on our purpose as Kingdom Writers.

The enemy can only know our thoughts if we speak them aloud or agree with them, so it's vital to guard our hearts and minds by taking those negative ideas captive. An unguarded mind can easily become a playground for distractions and temptations, leading us away from our true purpose and calling. The enemy wants us to think, "Why would God do this for me?" rather than realizing our worth by asking, "Why wouldn't God do this for me?" We need to be careful not to let discouraging thoughts take over, as they can pull us away from our writing. It's essential to evaluate whether our thoughts reflect God's truth, or if they are simply lies from the enemy. Always remember that feelings of condemnation come from the enemy, while God's gentle conviction leads us toward understanding and truth. As it says in

Romans 8:1, "Therefore, now no condemnation awaits those who are living in Jesus." Let this be your reminder to focus on the positive and fulfill your calling as a writer.

Many writers often feel overwhelmed by a flood of negative thoughts, doubts, and fears. This happens because the enemy aims to disrupt our creativity and the unique calling God has given us as writers. For example, someone who doesn't write might see clouds as nothing more than fluffy cotton balls floating in the sky. A writer, on the other hand, can take you into their world and show you amazing things through their words. They can make you see and feel what they do. A writer's response to describing clouds might look like this:

As the sun began its gentle descent beyond the horizon, a warm golden light enveloped the world, transforming it into a scene of tranquil beauty. As I sat in my seat by the window, my pen hovering expectantly above a blank page, waiting to capture the moment, my gaze wandered upward, drawn to the magnificent spectacle unfurling above. Fluffy white clouds danced gracefully, their edges kissed by hints of lavender and silver, swirling like elegant performers in a breathtaking ballet. Each movement sent ripples across the deepening indigo canvas of twilight, creating a visual symphony that stirred the heart.

For me, the second description urges me to think more and explore further, just like a writer's pulling you into their story can encourage readers to seek a deeper understanding of Christ. This is precisely what the enemy wishes to prevent. Proverbs 4:23 reminds us, "Guard your heart above all else, for it determines the course of your life." This verse encourages us to safeguard our minds against harmful thoughts. When a writer skillfully pens their words, they can take readers on a journey to new places. Writers not only create beautiful imagery but also have the power to lead others toward Christ by revealing the truth behind the lies that can ensnare us. This is why the enemy focuses on the thoughts of writers, trying to steer them away from their true purpose: to lead others closer to God through their writing.

WHEN WRITERS WORRY

Studies reveal that eighty to ninety percent of the things we worry about never actually happen, which means we waste a lot of our mental energy on thoughts that lead nowhere. Jesus offers us comfort in Matthew 11:28 when He says, "Come to me, all of you who are weary and carry heavy burdens, and I will give you rest." Many writers, like myself, often fear the unknown, especially when we plan our work ahead of time. While planning is useful, we must also stay open to the unexpected blessings God has in store for us. When feelings of not being good enough creep in, it's vital to refresh our minds with God's truth. The Bible encourages us to think about His Word, which helps us to see ourselves as conquerors and as precious creations, reminding us that each of us is His cherished favorite.

God wants us to be joyful and fully engaged in our calling. When we allow worry to distract us, we miss the inspiration and creativity that God wants to flow through us. In the Bible, Jesus talks about worry in a powerful way. In Luke 8:14, He points out that the seeds that fall among thorns represent people who hear His message but are soon choked by the worries and pleasures of life. This verse encourages us to recognize the dangers of letting our concerns overtake our minds. Just like those seeds, when we let our worries grow, they can prevent us from maturing in our writing.

Worry can cloud our thoughts, making it harder to see the beauty and purpose in our writing. Instead of focusing on our dreams and the messages we are inspired to share, we can find ourselves caught in a web of worry, fear, and doubt. Those distractions have a mission to make sure you turn from being a doer of the word to only a hearer of the word. Just as in the parable of the Sower. Remembering Matthew 13:3-8 can provide insight into how we can cultivate healthy thoughts. Just like a gardener tends to their plants, we must ensure our minds are free from distractions that hinder our growth. If we allow fears and insecurities to take over, we can easily forget the promises God has made for our lives. By presenting our worries to God, as encouraged in Philippians 4:6-7, we create fertile ground for hope and strength rather than anxiety. When we pray and ask for support, God fills us with peace that surpasses all understanding. This peace frees us to write joyfully, knowing that God is with us and that our work holds significance. As we create, we can remind ourselves that God is with us and that our work matters.

As writers, our minds can often become cluttered with worry and doubt. To help clear that clutter, we should turn to the wisdom found in Romans 12:1-2. This passage invites us to give both our bodies and minds to God. By doing so, we become living sacrifices, allowing Him to refresh our thoughts and change how we see things. It reminds us not to follow the paths of the world, which often leads to jealousy and comparison. As writers, it can be tempting to believe that if our work doesn't make a bestseller list, it isn't valuable. But this mindset distracts us from God's true calling for our lives. We must allow our minds to be renewed through prayer and the Word. However, renewing our minds isn't a passive process, it requires intentional action and vigilance, making sure that every thought aligns with God's truth and supports our calling as writers.

How do we practice this renewal? 2 Corinthians 10:3-5 reminds us that our battles are not against flesh and blood, but are spiritual in nature, fought not with human strength, but with the mighty power and authority that God provides. We are called to demolish strongholds and take our thoughts captive. Each thought presents a choice: Do we feed it with our attention and energy, or do we starve it and dismiss it? Examine how you treat those unhelpful thoughts. Let me ask you again, are you providing them with comfort like a cherished guest on your couch? Providing food and adjusting your thermostat to make sure they are comfortable? If so, it's time to show them to the door, and when they hesitate to leave, push them out and lock the door behind them. Our goal is to dominate our thoughts, making sure they serve our purpose and not hinder it. To truly master this process of mental renewal, we need practical tools and Scripture provides exactly that, offering us spiritual armor to protect and transform our minds for God's purposes.

There are many weapons in Scripture to help us take our thoughts captive. Ephesians 6 talks about the armor of God, which equips us to stand firm against the enemy's attacks. This armor includes the belt of truth, breastplate of righteousness, shoes of peace, shield of faith, helmet of salvation, and the sword of the Spirit, which is God's Word. The Greek word for "renew" signifies renovation, an act that transforms perceptions and perspectives, like renovating a room in your house. The idea is that after God renovates our minds, we will see the world and our writing, differently. Alongside equipping ourselves with spiritual armor and renewing our minds, it's just as important to build a supportive community around us, people who can encourage, pray, and walk with us as we pursue our writing calling.

It is also helpful to surround ourselves with supportive people who uplift us on our writing journey. Kingdom Writers can encourage each other to focus on faith and God's plans. Find a writing group or friends who can pray for you and share their experiences. They can remind you that you are not alone in your struggles. Together, you can lift each other up and stay focused on the important mission of spreading light through your writing. Remember that worry may come, but it doesn't have to control you. Embrace God's promises, seek His peace, and lean on your fellow Kingdom Writers for support. As you do, you will find that joy can blossom where worry once thrived. With every word you write, invite God into the process, and watch your creativity flourish. Allow your pen to be a tool that not only shares stories but also reflects His love and grace. The journey may not always be easy, but with faith and community, you can overcome worry and fulfill your calling.

As we move forward, it's important to pay attention to what we think about each day. Every little thought can turn into a bigger belief, which then affects how we act. To help keep our minds focused, we should set aside time daily to work on our writing goals. A great idea is to write down positive statements or affirmations and place them where we can easily see them. You could say things like, "I will write the book that God wants me to write," or "My words can help others." These reminders can guide us and keep us on track. We can learn from the parable of the Sower (Matthew 13:3-9), which teaches us about how important it is to take care of the good things we hear from God and let them grow in our hearts, just like we nurture our writing dreams. Doing this can help us entertain worry less and focus more on what truly matters.

In thinking about my own experiences, I remember a time when my house flooded. Instead of getting upset, my mother stayed calm and said, "God will take care of everything." Her ability to find peace during such unexpected and difficult times taught me a valuable lesson: trusting in God can lead to wonderful things, even when life is frustrating, challenging, or falling apart right before your eyes. These tough moments changed how I view challenges and sparked my love for writing again. Without that flood, this book more than likely would not have been written because I would not have been in the place I needed to be in order to write it. It wasn't until my mother passed that I started writing the book. Reflecting on this, I realized that even life's unexpected storms can become turning points that shift our perspective and renew our sense of purpose.

According to Philippians 4:6-7, we should not worry about anything. Instead, in every circumstance, we should bring our concerns to God through prayer and requests with a spirit of gratitude. When we do this, God's peace, which goes beyond our understanding, will protect our hearts and minds in Christ Jesus. This passage serves as a reminder that by entrusting our worries, especially the things we find heartbreaking to God, we can concentrate on what truly matters: loving God, loving others, and fulfilling God's perfect will for our lives. As we learn to surrender our worries to God and rest in His peace, it's also essential to recognize the influence our words and thoughts have on our well-being and our calling as writers.

Words, as we know, are profoundly significant; they possess the power of creation. Just like God spoke everything into being with a simple command in Genesis 1:3, where He said, "Let there be light," we too have the ability to speak life through what we say. Proverbs 18:21 teaches us, "The tongue can bring death or life; those who love to talk will reap the consequences." This reminds us of the importance of not focusing on worry but paying attention to our self-talk, the way we speak to ourselves. Are our thoughts and beliefs aligned with what God teaches? When our thoughts, words, and actions are in harmony with God's truth, we unlock the writer within us, revealing our full potential, as we navigate the challenges of worry and mental health. Recognizing the creative power of our words, we're reminded that

God works through our authentic selves, not some flawless ideal, so there's no need to let worry, or self-doubt hold us back from answering His call to write.

Why worry about a perfect, ideal version of yourself before you write? God has always used people just as they are, flaws and all. Think about Paul, who once was a persecutor of Christians, or Moses, who struggled with his confidence. Their stories remind us that everyone has imperfections, yet God still chose them to lead and inspire countless others. As writers, it's essential to break down our worries and doubts that may keep us from fulfilling our purpose. We need to capture every anxious thought and change it into something positive. This process of renewing our minds is ongoing, just as we learn in Romans 12:1-2, when we surrender our lives to God, we can discover what He truly wants for us. So, let's embrace our journeys, knowing that we can grow and write from our current selves, trusting in God's guidance. By shifting our perspective from self-doubt to God's promises, we can begin to challenge any thinking that doesn't reflect our true identity in Him.

Only by aligning our thoughts with God's truth can we uproot any beliefs that don't reflect our identity in Christ. The Bible reminds us in Romans 12:2 to "not be conformed to this world but be transformed by the renewing of your mind." When we do this, we can stop believing the lies that might creep into our thoughts. Think about how your thinking about writing affects your relationship with God. Does it draw you closer to His purpose for you, or does it push you away? By embracing mental transformation and renewal, we create a space that encourages creativity and helps us fulfill the special calling God has for our lives, which allows us to cultivate the fertile ground that fosters creativity and fulfills the call God has placed on our lives.

FIXING BAD THINKING HABITS

In the journey of writing, it's also essential to be aware of the ways we can trip ourselves up, especially when it comes to hindering our ability to express ourselves. One big challenge for many writers is thinking in ways that don't align with the teachings of the Bible. When our thoughts stray from these biblical standards, it can impact the quality of our writing. Additionally, if we view things negatively, we might miss out on many opportunities and struggle to unleash our creativity. It's important to reframe our thoughts toward positivity and hope; this allows our words to shine with warmth and clarity. Another habit that can hinder writers is when they overcomplicate their thoughts instead of keeping things simple. God created us with the ability to think clearly, and it's crucial that we embrace this gift! We should also be cautious of having a "my way or no way" mindset, as it can limit our openness to new ideas. Resisting change can block our growth and improvement, but if we welcome change, we can enhance our skills. Let us remain open and flexible, trusting in God's guidance as He leads us on our creative path. Remember, holding onto rigid thoughts can cause us to miss the wonderful messages that God wants us to express! It's not only our thinking that can hold us back; self-imposed limitations and comparisons can quietly stifle our growth as well.

Stereotyping ourselves is a habit that writers must be careful about. Sometimes, we limit our creativity by putting ourselves into tiny boxes filled with negative beliefs. When we remember that we are made in God's image (Genesis 1:27), we can start to break down these walls we've built in our minds. It's easy to get discouraged if we constantly compare ourselves to others. Instead, if we focus on the unique plan that God has for each of us and trust His timing, we can enjoy our own writing journey without feeling pressured to imitate someone else's. Each of us has a special purpose, and our writing can shine with that individuality, reflecting who we are. Remember, as it says in James 4:2-4, "You want what you don't have, so you scheme and kill to get it. You are jealous of what others have, but you can't get it, so you fight and wage war to take it away from them. Yet you don't have what you want because you don't ask God for it. And even when you ask, you don't get it because your motives are all wrong, you want only what will give you pleasure. You adulterers! Don't you realize that friendship with the world makes you an enemy of God? I say it again: If you want to be a friend of the world, you make yourself an enemy of God." When we become aware of these patterns and intentionally shift our focus, we create space for God's truth to reshape how we see ourselves and our creative work.

By shifting our perspective from self-doubt to God's promises, we can begin to challenge any thinking that doesn't reflect our true identity in Him. Setting healthy boundaries works to keep our thoughts in a good place. These boundaries act like a shield, protecting our minds from negative ideas and distractions that can interrupt our writing. Understanding who we are through the Bible can help us fill our minds with positive thoughts about our worth and purpose. For example, Ephesians 1 teaches us that we are loved by God. It's crucial for us to remind ourselves of this love regularly. These reminders can boost our confidence and spark our creativity. When we truly grasp our identity in Christ, we write from a place of strength and security, which makes our writing even more powerful. Remember, just as Philippians 4:8 encourages us to think about whatever is true, noble, and right, we must focus on these good thoughts to nurture our mental health as writers. As we strengthen these boundaries and regularly remind ourselves of our worth in Christ, it naturally leads us to develop habits, like practicing affirmations and forgiveness that further support a positive and resilient mindset.

To nurture and build a positive mindset, we should start practicing uplifting affirmations. For example, reminding ourselves that we are "difficult to offend" (Proverbs 19:1) can help us become more resilient. When we face criticism or negative comments, it's important to focus on our own truths. It's also crucial to be quick to forgive (Mark 11:25). This isn't just about our relationships with others; it also matters for how we think about ourselves. If we hold onto anger or let bitterness take over, our writing can feel heavy, gloomy, and confusing instead of bringing light, clarity, and inspiration. By learning to let go and forgive, we can create more joyful and engaging work. Letting go of negativity and embracing forgiveness not only lightens our own hearts but also opens the door for us to practice genuine love toward others.

Choosing to love others is a strong habit that can greatly improve our mental health as writers. Sometimes, it can be tempting to pull away from people or become negative, especially toward those we don't get along with well. However, we should remember to show kindness and love, just as it says in 1 John 4:19: "We love because he first loved us." When we do this, we build a sense of community and connection that boosts our creativity. When we write with love in our hearts, our words become more genuine and meaningful to those who read them. As Proverbs 16:24 says, "Kind words are like honey – sweet to the soul and healthy for the body." So, let's make it a habit to share love in our writing, and watch how it makes our work shine.

By developing these positive habits, we can change our thinking and become better writers. Each step we take brings us closer to understanding, inspiration, and creativity. This journey may take time and patience, but remember, God is with us every step of the way. As it says in Psalm 37:5, "Commit your ways to the Lord; trust in him and he will do this." Let's accept who we are meant to be in Him, allowing our writing to showcase His love and grace. As we work together with God, we will discover our unique voices and share stories that truly matter. So, write with confidence, think positively, and let your creativity shine like a light in the darkness, as Matthew 5:16 reminds us: "Let your light shine before others."

WRITER'S PHYSICAL HEALTH

Writers, especially those who identify as Kingdom Writers, often face a tough journey filled with hardships like depression, anxiety, and feelings of loneliness or isolation. These challenges can seriously affect their creativity, creating a cycle that makes it difficult to write. The enemy knows that if a writer is overwhelmed by these struggles, it can block the inspiration they need for their work. You may have heard of this being called "writer's block." That's why it's so important for Kingdom Writers to focus on their physical health. Our bodies are the temples that house our spirit to live and create on this Earth. If we let it fall apart through neglect, we might find ourselves unable to engage in the world we are so desperately needed in. Remember, we should not idolize our bodies, but we must take care of them so we can serve the Lord effectively in our writing and lives. The Bible offers wisdom on this topic. In 1 Corinthians 9:27, Paul says, "I discipline my body like an athlete, training it to do what it should. Otherwise, I fear that after preaching to others I myself might be disqualified." This reminds us that we must be the ones in charge of our bodies, not the other way around. When we neglect our health, it can feel like our bodies take over, limiting what we can do. It's easy to let discomfort, tiredness, or cravings for unhealthy food stop us from giving our best effort. Some writers may disregard their health by not eating properly, not getting enough sleep, or skipping exercise. Kingdom Writers need to stay strong and energetic so they can pursue their purpose without being held back by health problems that can be avoided with good nutrition, proper exercise, and rest.

Personally, I am facing several challenges as I try to improve my physical, mental, and spiritual health. I have lost just a little over one hundred pounds. However, I'm still not at my goal, and that's okay. Change doesn't happen overnight. It requires prayer, time, consistency, and dedication. However, I often struggle with society's pressures that tempt me to indulge in unhealthy lifestyles because it's cheaper to eat junk food or to prioritize work over necessary sleep and exercise. The world tells us that if we work hard enough now, we will eventually be rewarded with ease and comfort, allowing us to finally take care of ourselves. What the world fails to mention is that our bodies are like machines. If we push ourselves too hard, by the time we reach that so-called goal, we might find ourselves spending all our resources on repairing a body that is extremely worn down. It's important to remember not to let our bodies adapt to these messages from society, creating an internal reminder of what the world views as normal.

We must think about how our bodies communicate with us. Sometimes, we hear a small voice urging us to indulge in sugary snacks, skip a good night's sleep, or binge eat greasy foods. While it's true that our bodies can sway our decisions, it is essential to learn how to control these urges with discipline. This begins in our minds, where we hold the power to make wise choices. The Bible reminds us in 1 Corinthians 10:31 that whatever we eat or drink, or whatever we do, should be done to glorify God. When we take care of our bodies, we aren't just helping ourselves; we are honoring our Creator and improving our ability to share meaningful words with others. As writers who serve the Kingdom, we must realize that our physical health is closely connected to our creativity and writing skills. Feeling energetic and healthy can make our ideas and stories more lively and engaging. By committing to better care of our bodies, we not only improve our mood but also boost our creativity and reconnect with our purpose of spreading God's message. It can feel like a refreshing breeze that blows away feelings of doubt and sadness, allowing joy to shine through.

As writers who represent God's Kingdom, we must make physical health a top priority. Taking care of our bodies and minds prepares us to fulfill a greater purpose. Just as 1 Corinthians 6:19-20 reminds us that our bodies are temples, it is important to treat them with respect and care. By distancing ourselves from negative influences and adopting healthy habits, we empower our creativity. A writer's journey requires a strong, healthy body, and a vibrant spirit. Let's begin today! This can mean choosing a nutritious meal, going for a refreshing walk, or ensuring we get enough rest. Through discipline and intentionality, we can create a nurturing environment where our creativity can flourish and thrive. Together, we can embrace a lifestyle that supports our writing and enriches our lives.

———

CHAPTER 4 SUMMARY: THOUGHT LIFE AND ITS IMPORTANCE

This chapter emphasizes the critical role that our thoughts play in shaping our identity and purpose, particularly for writers who feel called to share God's message. We are likened to CEOs of our minds, as we have the power to manage our thoughts, especially when faced with negativity, self-doubt, and fear. The biblical principle from 2 Corinthians 10:5 encourages us to capture every thought to align it with Christ's truth.

We explore the dangers of entertaining negative thoughts, much like Eve in the Garden, and how these can distort our self-image and disrupt our creative flow. Hebrews 13:8 reassures us of God's unchanging nature, reminding us to cling to His truths rather than the lies that may cloud our vision.

We see an example of personal experiences of battling feelings of inadequacy, emphasizing the need for self-affirmation, and reliance on God's Word in Romans 8:16. With faith, we can embrace our identity as children of God who are called to be Kingdom Writers, cultivating an environment for creativity by ensuring our thoughts are rooted in positivity and truth.

Furthermore, the chapter discusses the significance of physical health in sustaining creativity and effectiveness in writing. By taking care of our bodies through proper nutrition and self-discipline, we honor God and enhance our ability to fulfill our calling.

ACTION STEPS

1. **Self-Reflection:** Regularly assess your thoughts and identify negative patterns that may be hindering your writing. Write them down so you can work through them.
2. **Scripture Affirmation:** Counter negative thoughts with relevant Scripture that speaks truth about your identity and purpose. For example, when you feel unqualified, refer to Philippians 4:19 to remind yourself of God's provision.
3. **Nurture a Positive Mental Environment:** Create a daily practice of positive affirmations related to your writing. Place them in visible areas to reinforce your calling as a Kingdom Writer.
4. **Physical Wellness Commitment:** Establish a routine that includes healthy eating, regular exercise, and adequate sleep. Consider simple actions like preparing nutritious meals or scheduling daily walks.
5. **Engage with Community:** Surround yourself with encouraging voices through fellowship with other writers and prayer groups. Share your experiences and challenges with trusted friends who uplift you.
6. **Pray for Strength and Guidance:** Daily invite God into your thought life and writing process. Seek His wisdom to renew your mind and redirect your creative efforts according to His will.

7. **Evaluate Writing Goals:** Set specific, actionable writing objectives that reflect your unique voice as a Kingdom Writer. Regularly review and adjust these goals to stay aligned with your purpose.

By integrating these practices into your life, you will enable growth in your writing journey, anchored by a strong mental and physical foundation rooted in faith.

CHAPTER 5
Our Responsibility

OUR RESPONSIBILITY AS WRITERS

AS WRITERS, we have an incredible responsibility that comes with our calling. It's important to acknowledge that the path of a writer isn't always simple; it's not just about sitting down and letting words mindlessly flow. 1 Peter 5:8 warns us that the enemy loves to invade our minds and twist our thoughts away from God's truth. Reflecting on our calling, we might wonder, what if the very people we are meant to lead to Christ are waiting for us on the other side of the words we write? It's a profound thought that should inspire us to write so those very people can find us. Matthew 5:16 reminds us to let our light shine so others may see our good deeds and glorify God. The truth of the matter is we do not fit in with the world because our divine purpose requires us to stand out and connect with those searching for hope.

As Kingdom Writers, we have a responsibility to truly understand our purpose and to listen for God's guidance in our work. The Bible tells us in Psalm 46:10, "Be still, and know that I am God." This reminds us to silence the noise around us, especially the distractions of social media, which can be overwhelming. Sometimes, we need to step back, even from our friends, to focus on what God wants us to hear.

For me, this meant taking two years to intentionally quiet my mind so I could truly listen for God's voice. During that season, I chose not to speak with friends or spend time on social media. Instead, I dedicated myself to learning how to be still and studying the Word, allowing God to teach me how to listen to Him more deeply. It was during those quiet moments that I began to understand His plans for me as a writer. Now, on the other hand, it's easy to think we must make everything super serious. However, Ecclesiastes 3:1-8 tells us:

> "For everything there is a season, a time for every activity under heaven. A time to be born, and a time to die; a time to plant, and a time to harvest; a time to kill, and a time to heal; a time to tear down, and a time to build up; a time to cry, and a time to laugh; a time to grieve, and a time to dance. A time to scatter stones, and a time to gather them; a time to embrace, and a time to turn away; a time to search, and a time to quit searching; a time to keep, and a time to throw away; a time to tear, and a time to mend; a time to be quiet, and a time to speak; a time to love, and a time to hate; a time for war, and a time for peace."

These verses remind us that life has different seasons, and as writers, we need to recognize when it is time to be quiet in the wilderness so we can listen and hear God and know when God says it is time to share our words with the world. By embracing this balance, we can fulfill our responsibility as writers and gain a deeper understanding of our unique calling.

Embracing our roles thoughtfully allows us to appreciate the creative process more deeply. Proverbs 10:5 reminds us of the importance of recognizing the season we're in. Like a wise youth who harvests during summer, we need to seize the moments we have to grow. Every season brings its own challenges and triumphs, and reflection is key in navigating them. When mistakes happen, it's vital to express gratitude for God's forgiveness and keep moving forward. Avoid the trap of "I should have" or "I could have." Instead, let's shift our mindset by renewing our thoughts to align with our standing in God, which encompasses our identity as His beloved children.

As Kingdom Writers, we must also resist the temptation to compare our work with that of others. While we can learn valuable lessons from fellow writers, remember that no one else can share our story in the same way we can. Each one of us is a unique creation of God, created for a special purpose and entrusted with an important message. As it is written in Psalm 139:14, "I praise you because I am fearfully and wonderfully made." If we try to copy someone else's style or story, we risk losing our unique voice. Instead of allowing comparison to fill our hearts, we should practice self-affirmation. Whenever you look in the mirror, take a moment to say, "Thank you, God, for making me a unique individual with a purpose." This small act can help remind you of your special identity as a child of God. Nowadays, social media can make it easy to fall into the trap of comparison, which may leave us feeling inadequate. If you find yourself constantly checking on what others have accomplished, it might be wise to take a break from those distractions. Each moment spent scrolling is a moment that could be spent writing. Focus your energy on what God has specifically designed you to express. It is also important to celebrate the achievements of other writers from the heart, rather than letting jealousy creep in. By keeping our thoughts aligned with positivity, we can protect ourselves from negative influences. As we embrace our individuality and our calling, we can fully honor the responsibility we have as writers.

As Kingdom Writers, we must recognize that sharing God's message is a unique and special privilege. In other words, we do not just write whenever we feel like it. Writing is a valuable gift that requires our effort and dedication. Even when we do not have the strength to pick up our pens and write, we must write. However, it's also natural to desire recognition for our efforts. Sometimes, we want others to praise us for following our instructions and sharing our stories. Although there is nothing wrong with telling our personal experiences, we must be cautious. Proverbs 27:2 teaches us, "Let another praise you, and not your own mouth; a stranger, and not your own lips." When the spotlight shifts from God to ourselves, we must remember that our writing should ultimately reflect His glory, not our own achievements. Our responsibility as writers is to inspire others while keeping our focus on the message we are sharing and the greater purpose it serves, which is to honor and glorify God and not ourselves.

One of the greatest challenges as a writer is to raise the quality of our writing by connecting it with God's truth rather than simply following the trends of the world. To achieve this, we need to explore the Scriptures deeply and allow the Holy Spirit to help us understand their meaning. We do this by reading the Bible regularly. This practice not only strengthens our own faith but also enriches the messages we share with others. As it says in 2 Timothy 3:16-17, "All Scripture is God-breathed and is useful for teaching, rebuking, correcting and training in righteousness, so that the servant of God may be thoroughly equipped for every good work."

By focusing on God's Word, we can fulfill our responsibility as writers to convey truth and hope. While it's great to read books and commentaries about the Bible, nothing compares to engaging with the Scriptures directly. When we read the Bible, our faith is increased (Romans 10:17). Overall, we must ensure that our spirits, souls, and bodies are in harmony with God's will, enabling us to hear His instructions. The voices we hear can be confusing, but as Kingdom Writers, being rooted in God's Word will help us clearly discern His voice. Make it a daily practice to communicate with God through prayer, meditate on His Word, and seek His direction.

As Kingdom Writers, we are ambassadors for God, sharing His message and values through our writing. Our responsibility goes beyond just writing or speaking on big stages. It actually begins in our personal lives, where God is shaping us every day. Our writing should show God's love and light to others. Before we put our words out into the world, it's important for us to recognize how God is working in our lives. Writing should always honor Him, and every word we write should feel like a special gift we are giving back to God to glorify Him. Colossians 3:23 says, "Work willingly at whatever you do, as though you were working for the Lord rather than for people," reminding us to focus on making our writing a true reflection of our faith.

We must act proactively, pursuing the audiences God has called us to reach, never waiting for them to find us. When God nudges us to write about something important, it's essential we respond without hesitation. Our creative energies need to follow God's lead, and we are tasked with finding unique ways to connect with those who do not know Him. Every writer has a distinct purpose; for example, some encourage, while others warn or inspire imagination. As Kingdom Writers, we must recognize that we are part of a larger community brought together by God. Just like an oak tree with strong, deep roots, our faith can grow robust and unwavering, allowing God's anointing to flow through us. To become the writers that God has intended us to be, we need to prepare ourselves, be patient, and be open to His guidance in our hearts and minds.

It is important for us to earnestly seek the truth found in the Scriptures. We should approach our writing with the goal of gaining greater understanding and building faith not only in ourselves but also in our readers. Our goal here is to strive to fulfill our responsibilities as writers for God's Kingdom, using our talents to inspire and uplift others. As we step forward in obedience and creativity, our commitment to reaching others becomes a living testimony of our faith, one that not only fulfills our calling but also invites others to experience God's love and truth through the written word.

Writing is a powerful way to share the knowledge of Christ with others, either directly or indirectly. It's like offering an invitation to experience the hope we have found in Him. In John 15:4-5, we learn that staying close to Jesus is very important; without Him, we can do nothing. Our writing reflects our relationship with Christ. Through our words, we can guide others to align their lives with God's teachings. Let us embrace our roles as Kingdom Writers. We have the responsibility to reach out with encouragement, to bring hope, and to uplift others through the stories we tell. Writing in a way that spreads His love and truth brings this Scripture to life.

FINDING YOUR PLACE TO GROW AS A WRITER

Every writer needs a special place to grow their skills and improve their craft, especially when writing for God's kingdom. The journey begins with a commitment to daily reading and prayer. For me, this commitment was not as easy as it seems. As an outreach pastor with a degree in theology, I studied Scripture daily for others but often forgot to engage with it for my own heart. I could stand in front of crowds, sharing the importance of studying the Word, wearing my accomplishments like badges of honor. However, one day, I heard a gentle voice urging me to take my own advice seriously. After weeks of reflection, I realized I had been studying for others and not nurturing my relationship with God's Word. This realization led me to pray earnestly about my relationship with God.

As writers, we must understand that our first mission is to connect with God personally. If we are only sharing His love without experiencing it ourselves, we miss out on the most important part of our journey. God desires a personal relationship with each of us, and that connection fuels our creativity. Imagine being like a grand ship with a purpose to travel the world carrying precious resources, our words. These words can touch lives profoundly, but only if we first fill ourselves with God's love. When we release our work into the world, we must remember that we do not determine where it goes. God is the captain of our journey, guiding our thoughts and navigating the ideas he has given us to unexpected places. This is an exciting adventure that calls for us to trust in His timing and purpose. With this new awareness, our next step is to make Scripture personal and relevant to our own journeys as writers.

Once we immerse ourselves in Scripture, it's crucial to personalize what we read. A powerful exercise is to take verses that speak to our current struggles and insert our names into them. For example, if I am fearful, I would take 2 Timothy 1:7 and say, "Charis, God has not given you a spirit of fear." It's a simple yet effective way to remind ourselves that God is speaking directly to us. This interactive way of reading creates an intimate conversation with God. After this step, prayer becomes our next tool. It's essential to be honest in these moments of prayer, asking for understanding and clarity about our hearts and minds. One of my go-to prayers comes from Ephesians 1:18, where I ask God to open the eyes of my heart to understand His incredible hope for me. Yet, while nurturing our individual relationship with God is foundational, we must also recognize that our journey is meant to be shared with the wider body of Christ.

We were never meant, nor were we designed, to handle everything by ourselves. Many members make up the body of Christ, and only one head, which is Jesus. I lived in a fantasy world for many years when it came to this subject, thinking I needed to do everything. Sometimes, it's easy to feel as if we need to handle everything ourselves, just like I did when I was the pastor of my old church's Celebrate Recovery ministry. I worked tirelessly, thinking that if I didn't lead every aspect, nothing would get done right, and everything had to be done in excellence. However, God showed me the joy of delegation; He has equipped many others to serve alongside me, and their gifts were way better than mine. Together, we created something only God could create. The same concept carries over to our writing endeavors. We need to appreciate that we are not the sole operators on this grand journey; we're part of a supportive community. While I have put considerable effort into writing and publishing this book, many others have worked behind the scenes to ensure it reaches you. The Holy Spirit often encourages us to depend on our fellow brothers and sisters in Christ. Ignoring these prompts can prevent others from showcasing their God-given talents and can deprive your audience of the opportunity to read your book.

As we continue our journey, let's remember that writing is about enjoying the process, not just focusing on the end goal. Each paragraph we write is a steppingstone to discovering our unique voice and message. Every challenge teaches us new lessons that can enrich our writing and strengthen our connection to God. Let's set aside time each day to read, reflect, and pray. God desires us to flourish as writers, and through His guidance, we can create works that inspire and uplift others. Like beautiful trees planted by flowing waters, our words can bear fruit that nourishes the souls of those who encounter them. Trusting in God's timing allows us to thrive in His perfect plan, encouraging us to write boldly from our hearts. May we all embrace the journey as we grow and cultivate our gifts as writers, sharing the incredible story of God's love with the world around us.

MEDITATING AND SPENDING TIME IN THE WORD

Have you ever wondered how to really change your thoughts? One of the best ways to do this is by meditating on God's Word. We touched on this in the last chapter, but let's dive deeper into what it means to meditate on the scriptures. Meditation involves taking time to think carefully about what we read in the Bible, usually in quiet, so we can let the words touch our hearts. It's like having a gentle conversation within ourselves that brings clarity and understanding. God's Word reveals who we are to Him, and when we view ourselves through His eyes, it can completely change how we see ourselves.

Just as Jesus went into the wilderness to connect with God before starting His ministry, we also need quiet time with the Lord to prepare for our own writing journey. Remember that, like Jesus faced temptations in the wilderness, we will encounter our own struggles too. In Matthew 4, we see how Jesus used Scripture to resist the devil's temptations. He didn't just stand firm once; He fought back three times by quoting God's Word. This reminds us that when challenges arise, we should turn to the Bible for comfort and guidance.

From my own experience, I understand the importance of stepping back to heal and focus on writing. I've dealt with my own distractions along the way, especially from media, which can pull us away from reading the Bible. It's important to be aware that distractions are trying to keep us from the life-changing teachings found in God's Word. When we let other things fill our lives instead of focusing on God, we risk allowing the world to tell us who we are, and this is what our flesh craves. We may start to see ourselves through societal labels rather than through God's eyes. Some of you might think I'm criticizing media, and that's not my intention. However, we need to recognize how distractions can lead us away from God. When we spend more time-consuming worldly content than studying the Bible, it can alter our self-perception and lead us to share messages that conflict with God's truth in our writing.

Consider this analogy: If I told you I had a trunk filled with ten million dollars in gold, wouldn't you be excited to see it? You'd want to open it and explore the treasure inside. Now, imagine being told that this trunk would never close, and you could take as much gold as you wanted. You would probably invite your family and friends to share in this incredible fortune. If you're anything like me, you'd be in a rush to grab as much as possible, just in case the chance disappeared! But what if I told you that you possess something far more valuable than the gold in that trunk? The Bible is like a treasure chest, filled with wisdom and guidance that helps us grow closer to God. The Bible tells the greatest love story of all, how Jesus gave Himself up so we could have a lasting relationship with God. Our Heavenly Father made everything, even the most valuable things like gold. You might be thinking, "I already know this," but my question is, do your actions show this belief? I strongly believe that actions speak louder than words. So, what do your actions say about how important God's Word is in your life?

As writers, we must embrace and apply God's Word in our writing. But how do we do this? First, we need to spend time in the Bible, looking for what God wants us to share through our work. Being intentional with our reading helps us understand His love and character, strengthening our connection to Him. When we recognize who has chosen us and the purpose behind our calling, we can become instruments of His will. Seeking His guidance is crucial for understanding what He wants us to convey in our writing. As we read the Bible, we learn about God's love, His character, and His voice. This personal connection to His Word not only deepens our relationship with Him but also enhances our ability to share our stories with others. In 1 John 4:19, it says, "We love because He first loved us." This reminds us that our writing can reflect that love to the world.

BECOMING SENSITIVE TO GOD'S INSTRUCTION THROUGH HIS WORD

A story comes to mind about a young woman who passionately dreams about helping flowers. But when she turns to God's Word, she feels led to focus instead on bees. At first, this confuses her. How can focusing on bees connect to her love for flowers? Yet, God often has a bigger plan for her than she can see right away. In this young woman's case, she wants to celebrate the beauty of flowers, not realizing that

God is guiding her to a new calling as a beekeeper. Through her dedication to bees, she learns about their vital role in pollination, which helps flowers grow. This shows God's extraordinary wisdom by channeling her love for flowers in a new way, where she finds joy and purpose. As she masters the art of beekeeping, she realizes she is not only living out her dream but also encouraging others to appreciate bees and their effect on flowers and plants. Through her efforts, she aids in pollination, which is essential for many plants to grow and produce food. This is an excellent way to help her community, as bees play a crucial role in pollinating plants, which in turn provide oxygen. Now she plays a bigger role with bees, where together they nurture the environment and support life on our planet.

Just like the beekeeper, we must remember that we don't have to know everything when answering God's call to write. Accepting that we don't have all the answers allows God to work wonders through us. Writing is about growth, and learning from Scripture provides a strong foundation. When we are open to God's lessons, we become more aware of how He can use our stories. Being humble and receptive to His guidance, as suggested in John 9:39, helps us avoid the blindness of thinking we know it all. By staying humble, we can uncover our true purpose as writers, with God's loving guidance lighting our path.

A commitment to spending time in God's Word to discover the beauty of His purpose for our lives is mandatory. We have the power to create change, inspire others, and reveal God's handiwork in the world through our writing. Just like the young woman discovers that her passion for flowers can bloom through beekeeping, we too can find our own paths illuminated through Scripture. By nurturing our relationship with God, we open the door to extraordinary opportunities and the possibility of fulfilling our divine purposes alongside the desires of our hearts. With faith, we can embrace the journey ahead, knowing that with God in our hearts, we are equipped to bless those around us.

PLANNING

When it comes to spending time with the Lord, being honest with ourselves is the first step in setting a meaningful plan. It's easy to get caught up in what others might do; however, God desires for us to build our own relationship with Him based on our personal journey, not someone else's. It's ok to commit to smaller goals. Spending just fifteen minutes a day in dedicated practice can be a meaningful start, especially when approached with sincerity and purpose. God can take those fifteen minutes of intentional devotion to nurture our hearts and spirits, readying us for the blessings to come. Just as a seed develops into a strong tree over time, our spiritual habits will also flourish when we tend to them daily. I have witnessed many times how fifteen minutes with the Lord can lead to hours that you don't even realize the time has gone by. However, this growth depends on your own desire, not anyone else's.

As Kingdom Writers, it's essential for us to immerse ourselves in God's Word, but this can only happen if we form consistent habits. Before we dive into any plans, we must reflect on how reliable our word is when it comes to our commitments. Ask yourself, *Do I keep my promise to write, even when faced with challenges?* For example, imagine God prompts you to write out Scripture over the weekend, but someone offers you $300 and dinner to help them move instead. It's tempting, especially if you urgently need money and the move will only take up a couple hours of your day. If you're only considering the financial gain and ignoring God's call, you have to ask where your priorities truly lie. If someone asked you to do the same task for free, would your commitment to God still stand strong? If Jesus knocked on your door and asked to see the Scripture you read or wrote, how would you feel explaining why you hadn't written or read anything? Would you say you chose $300 and a pizza over doing what He asked? These reflections help us examine our hearts and our priorities in this beautiful journey called life.

It's important to recognize how our choices reflect our love and commitment to God. Each time we choose to prioritize earthly matters over our divine calling, we risk telling Jesus that His commands are second best to our desires for comfort or financial security. These choices are often subtle but, over time, can lead to weakening our walk with Him. We are not just accountable for what we choose to do, but also for what we choose to neglect. How much more fulfilling to tell Jesus that we wrote, even if it meant sacrificing a bit of comfort! Every moment spent in obedience to Him is a moment well-spent, and those moments build up to a glorious testimony. Let us remember that every "yes" we say to our calling is a testament to our relationship with Him.

Ultimately, it's crucial to let our words hold weight. In Matthew 5:37, we are reminded to let our "yes" be a true commitment and our "no" be resolute as well. When it comes to our writing journey, every promise we make, both to ourselves and to God, matters. Choose to treat your gift and anointing with the respect they deserve by putting them first and committing to God's call with all your heart. Every time we write, we honor God and uplift ourselves in the process. So, as you plan your days, remember that taking small steps consistently over time leads to extraordinary growth. As we build our lives around spending time with the Lord and pursuing our calling as writers, let's be gentle with ourselves while also being intentional. Starting with just fifteen minutes a day can lead to amazing transformations in our spiritual life and our writing. As we keep our commitments and prioritize our relationship with God, He will guide us and bless our efforts. We are part of His wonderful tapestry, and every thread of our faithfulness contributes to His great design. So let us take courage, extend ourselves grace, and make a firm commitment to honor our gifts as we journey forward with love and purpose.

EMBRACE AND APPLY GOD'S WORD

Embracing and applying God's Word is a meaningful habit for every writer. As we weave our thoughts and experiences into words, it is vital to understand how those words can reflect God's presence in our lives. 1 Corinthians 14:12 encourages us to seek gifts that uplift the entire church. This not only applies to our writing but reminds us that our words hold power and can inspire those who read them. When God nudges us to write, we must answer that call with eagerness and courage, recognizing that our writing has the potential to impact current and future generations. We are all part of a larger Kingdom story, and our unique voices can lead others to feel God's love and grace. Understanding this, we can look to Scripture for powerful examples of how words, when spoken or written in obedience to God, have the capacity to shape reality and illuminate the world.

Words are incredibly important, and the Bible teaches us about their power. With the entire Bible being filled with transformative, life-changing words, God shows us just how vital our speech and writing are. Words matter a lot, and the Bible shows us how powerful they can be. The entire Bible is a wonderful collection of God's words that can change our lives, and they tell us just how important writing is. Imagine if none of the Kingdom Writers in the Bible listened to God when He told them to write. What if they were too busy or didn't have the time? We wouldn't know anything about God! However, because of their obedience, we can read the Bible and see it is truly a masterpiece of God's words, guiding us to understand and share His message. One of the many profound examples comes from Genesis 1:3, where God declares, "Let there be light." And just like that, light emerged. This moment showcases the creative power of words; they can bring forth life and goodness, separating light from darkness. As writers, we must understand that our words can shine brightly, offering hope and clarity to those who feel lost or in despair. When we commit to penning our thoughts, we too become agents of light in a world that often feels shrouded in darkness.

However, the journey of a writer isn't always smooth. Many of us find ourselves craving validation, especially from book reviews. It's easy to let feedback define our worth as writers, as I once did. I vividly remember receiving a review on my first book that simply said, "You need to write more." Instead of seeing this as constructive criticism, I interpreted it as a personal attack on my abilities. This experience led me to stop writing for almost a year. Similar to the story in Genesis 3, where the serpent twists God's words to deceive Eve, we too can fall prey to deceptive thoughts that undermine our confidence. We must take care not to allow negative words to take root in our hearts and suffocate our creativity. But it's not just public feedback that can shake our confidence; often, the words of friends, family, or our own self-doubt can have an even deeper impact.

It's vital to recognize the twisted words that can come from both outside and within. Often, those closest to us may unintentionally cast doubt on our gifts and aspirations. They may link our writing to our past struggles or current responsibilities, saying things like, "Oh, but you had difficulties in school." Such comments can carry the weight of our family's expectations, leaving us feeling that the only path is the one they deem acceptable. In these moments, we must remember our calling. As writers, we are tasked with sharing our truths with the world, even when it feels scary or when others question our journey. We must declare, "My faith gives me the strength to pursue this dream, not my limitations or my past." We must embrace our scars and imperfections while writing as badges of honor, for God can transform them into something beautiful.

The battlefield of writing is often filled with distractions and doubts. Let me expand on what I mentioned earlier. The parable of the Sower in Luke 8 beautifully illustrates the different ways people respond to God's Word. In this passage, some seeds fall along the path and are quickly snatched away by the enemy, while others start to grow but wither soon after because they lack deep roots. As writers, we might start with enthusiasm, but life's temptations and challenges, the cares, riches, and pressures of daily life can crowd out our passion. We might hesitate to pursue our calling because we're overwhelmed by responsibilities or distractions. Yet, God's Word urges us to deepen our roots, to remain steadfast despite the worries that may try to divert us. In difficult times, it might feel like writing is an impossible task, especially when facing grief and other life challenges. Yet in these challenging moments, it is essential to hold onto God's promise. Luke 8:15 illustrates this beautifully by comparing the seeds sown on good soil to those who possess a noble and good heart. These individuals hear the Word, keep it close, and through their perseverance, they yield a fruitful harvest. No matter our circumstances, if we hold tightly to our calling as writers, letting faith guide us, we can begin to produce a literary ministry that leads others to Christ. Remember, our challenges can fuel our creativity, and our stories can provide hope to others who may be experiencing similar hardships.

Reflecting on my own experiences, I recall the wisdom shared during a women's Bible study in my twenties. A member stated that the Bible is a unique book because, as you read it, it reads you, too. This insight resonated deeply with me as I began to apply Scripture to every part of my life, including my writing journey. Whether I was feeling encouraged, distracted, or fearful, there was always a verse that spoke to my situation. Each time God directed my heart, it challenged me to reflect on my beliefs. Have you ever felt called to give but hesitated due to financial worries? Or felt excited to share your thoughts but got sidetracked by life's demands? God's Word remains our manual for navigating such moments.

As we engage in the writing process, we must remember that each struggle we face can be a lesson in resilience and faith. Just as God's Word guides us, our written words can offer guidance and consolation to those who need it. Let us commit to not allowing doubt or fear to silence our voices. Each of us is gifted uniquely, and when we embrace and apply God's Word, we become part of His divine narrative. Our job is to articulate our truth and God's love through our writing, making visible the invisible grace that He showers upon us each day.

Embracing and applying God's Word as writers is a journey of faith, courage, and self-discovery. When we face challenges, let us remind ourselves that our voices matter. God has a purpose for our lives, and our words can transcend generations, bringing light into the darkness. So, as we pick up our pens and open our hearts, let us remember the power we hold in sharing our stories. Whenever God calls us to write, let us answer with enthusiasm and determination, trusting that He will guide our efforts and bless our words, making them fruitful for His Kingdom.

THE RESPONSIBILITY OF FAITH FOR KINGDOM WRITERS

Faith is a key part of our journey as Kingdom Writers. It helps us understand who God is and what He has called us to do. You might ask yourself, "How can I write if I'm not sure about my abilities?" The answer is simple: God is our provider. His love wraps around us like a warm blanket, and even when we can't see it, we need to believe that He has given us everything we need to succeed. In Philippians 4:6-8, we are encouraged not to worry but to pray about everything. When we talk to God about our needs and thank Him for what He has done, we will find a peace that protects our hearts and minds. This belief is the beginning of our faith journey.

As Kingdom Writers, we have to learn how to shift our thinking. We need to focus on what God says. Our thoughts can either help us believe in our calling or make us doubt it. For instance, believing "I am a talented Kingdom Writer" brings joy to God, while the opposite thought can weaken our faith. Hebrews 11:1 reminds us, "Faith shows the reality of what we hope for; it is the evidence of things we cannot see." Therefore, it's important to pay attention to our thoughts and recognize their power over our faith.

As Kingdom Writers, every word we write should spring from faith. If you can't speak words of faith, it's better to hold your tongue. Faith is crucial not just for success in writing but also as a measure of our obedience to God. When He calls us to write, it requires faith to step into that calling. God delights in our faith, especially when we act without needing constant encouragement. Like Abraham, who left everything based on God's promise, we too must write with confidence when God instructs us. Remember, nothing is too hard for our Lord! Like exercising, take small steps in faith so your writing "muscles" grow stronger over time. When God tells us to write, we can trust that He will give us the tools we need.

It's important to know that faith and grace go hand in hand. Faith is how we respond to God's grace; it's how we receive the good things God has in store for us. Every time we write, we need faith. Each word and sentence we write is an act of trust in God. If we don't have faith in our words, we should not be sharing them. Every decision we make shows how much we believe in God's promises. As Kingdom Writers, we not only speak about our values and beliefs, but we also actively practice and embody them. Remember, God loves our faith even when we stand alone, just as Abraham did when he obeyed God's command.

We must also respond to His call with faith, truly believing that

God is guiding our writing journey, even when we can't see the full picture. As we move forward, challenges are bound to arise, bringing moments of doubt, fear, or uncertainty that can make us question our purpose. In these times, our faith isn't meant to shrink; it's meant to grow stronger and more resilient. Writing, like any discipline, can feel like lifting heavy weights sometimes. It stretches us, pushes us beyond our comfort zones, and requires effort and perseverance. Just as our physical muscles need regular exercise to become stronger, our faith needs to be stretched and strengthened through practice and trust.

When God asks us to take a step, whether it's starting a new project, sharing our testimony, or simply writing with honesty and vulnerability, it's natural to feel nervous or even afraid. But stepping out in faith, even when it feels scary, is an act of obedience that honors God. We can rest assured that nothing is too difficult for Him. He is with us in every moment, encouraging us to take things one step at a time. We don't have to rush or have it all figured out; we just need to trust Him with each part of the process.

As we spend time in His Word, we gain wisdom, encouragement, and direction. When we act on our testimonies and the insights given to us by the Holy Spirit, it's like picking up a sword and preparing for what lies ahead. Each act of faith, no matter how small, equips us for the next challenge and strengthens our ability to serve others through our writing. The more we practice listening to God and following His lead, the more confident we become in our calling.

Remember, every step of faith you take is meaningful. God honors your willingness to trust Him, and He uses your obedience to make an impact far beyond what you can see. So, let's continue to move forward, relying on His strength, and allowing our faith to grow with every word we write.

Positive speech is essential for us as Kingdom Writers because the words we use have a direct impact on our mindset, our faith, and even the fruitfulness of our writing journey. When we complain or speak negatively, whether about our progress, our abilities, or the challenges we face, we can unintentionally slow down our faith journey and create unnecessary obstacles for ourselves. It's important to always remember that our words are powerful; they can either build up or tear down, encourage or discourage, move us forward or keep us stuck. Speaking poorly about our situations or doubting what God has placed inside us only holds us back from fully stepping into the purpose and calling He has for us. Instead, we must choose to fight for our faith, even when it feels like the world is against us, and especially when others doubt our abilities or tell us "no." In those moments, it's vital to hold on to the truth that God says "yes", His approval and promises matter far more than any opinion or rejection we might encounter. Writing itself can be an incredible expression of faith, a way to declare God's goodness and share hope with others, but it also requires us to face our challenges honestly. Faith doesn't mean pretending difficulties don't exist; rather, it gives us the courage and strength to deal with them while continuing to trust in God's goodness, timing, and faithfulness. By choosing positive, faith-filled speech, we not only encourage ourselves but also inspire others, allowing our words to become a source of light and hope in a world that desperately needs it.

As Kingdom Writers, it is important to be comfortable with who you are, embracing the unique qualities God has given you and recognizing that your individuality is a gift meant to shine through your words. Many writers struggle with self-doubt, wrestling with feelings of inadequacy or the temptation to imitate others who seem more successful or confident. However, the true power of your writing comes when you choose to celebrate your own story, your voice, and the special perspective God has placed within you. Instead of measuring yourself against others or trying to fit into someone else's mold, focus on developing a deep love for the God who created you and trust that He has equipped you for your specific calling. Writing from an authentic place—where your heart, faith, and experiences are fully present, will not only bring you greater fulfillment but also draw others closer to Christ, as they encounter truth, vulnerability, and hope through your words. Remember, faith is more than just a list of beliefs written on a page; it comes alive in our actions, our obedience, and our willingness to step out even when it feels uncomfortable. Romans 10:17 reminds us that faith comes from hearing the Word of God, so let's make it a daily practice to soak in His truths, allowing them to inspire, guide, and strengthen us as we write. By embracing who you are and letting God's Word shape your journey, you'll find the courage to write boldly and the grace to impact lives in ways you may never have imagined.

It's also important to remember that faith is a daily lifestyle and not just something we turn to in hard times. Real faith is about consistently choosing to trust God's promises, no matter what our circumstances or emotions may tell us. It means understanding the realities of the world around us yet deciding to lean on God's truth rather than being driven by our feelings or doubts. Abraham's unwavering faith in God's promises, even when he couldn't see how things would work out, stands as a powerful example for us, he believed without seeing, and God honored that faith. In the same way, our commitment to walking in faith, especially when we face challenges or uncertainty, is what will lead us to true success as Kingdom Writers. Romans 1:17 reminds us, "It is through faith that a righteous person has life." When we make faith a daily practice, trusting God in both the ordinary and the difficult moments, we empower ourselves to fulfill the unique purpose He has given us. This daily walk of faith enables us to share God's hope and truth through our writing, impacting others and advancing His kingdom with every word we write.

THE RESPONSIBILITY OF OBEDIENCE FOR KINGDOM WRITERS

Obedience is an important word that often makes us pause and consider who truly has influence in our lives, are we allowing God to guide our steps, or are we swayed by the opinions and expectations of others? John 5:44 challenges us with these words: "No wonder you can't believe! For you gladly honor each other, but you don't care about the honor that comes from the one who alone is God." This scripture reminds us that our focus should be on seeking God's approval above all else, rather than chasing after the praise and validation of people.

When we choose to write or create from a place of obedience, our work becomes more than just words on a page; it is shaped by a purpose that aligns with God's kingdom and brings glory to Him. As authors, we are called to share messages that touch hearts, encourage transformation, and inspire others to draw closer to God. Embracing God's desire for obedience as writers is not just an outward act but a journey of the heart. It requires us to listen deeply, trust fully, and let His will guide both our creative process and the impact of our words.

Throughout the years, I have participated in many writing workshops and events, and they all share a similar message: If God has called you to write a book, then go ahead and write it! I felt proud of my achievements as an author who had written a several books whenever I heard the speaker say, "Write the book." But I noticed something troubling in the audience. Even with all the clapping and excitement, there seemed to be a lack of support and community that writers need. There were no seeds planted, no nurturing water to grow ideas, and no harvest to gather from the efforts of aspiring writers. Instead, I witnessed a cycle of inspiration that didn't lead to real results. That's when the Holy Spirit spoke to me, highlighting that my applause was hollow if I wasn't serving those around me who were eager to create. It was time for me to step up and write not just for myself, but for others, to help them expand the Kingdom via their call to write. Despite my insecurities, fear, and discomfort, I chose not to assist anyone, and instead concentrated solely on my own project, whatever it may be for that day. As long as I'm writing, I suppose that makes me somewhat obedient, right? The answer is no.

One Sunday, a couple of years ago, during church, I felt a powerful presence of the Holy Spirit. In that moment, I became sensitive to and aware of how much pride and disobedience I often let lead my life. Even though I had written and published books, worked on writing projects, and helped other writers through groups, I still felt distracted and unsure of myself. I wondered if I was good enough to help others on their writing paths. I would tell myself that if they saw I had written and published a book, that should be enough to inspire them to write too. In my mind it was enough because it was in close proximity to what God asked me to do. Surely, God wouldn't choose someone like me and expect me to write a collection of books telling writers all my struggles when I write. Nor would he want me to write while in the midst of those struggles, right? Wrong, because every word you've read in this book so far, was written while I was in the midst of my own struggles. There were struggles that made me question every single day whether writing this collection was even worth it. I often wondered if anyone would care about what I had to say, or if my words would truly make a difference in someone's life.

If you are facing similar feelings of doubt, know that you are not alone. It is essential to recognize that many of us struggle with self-doubt. Just as it says in Proverbs 16:18, "Pride goes before destruction, and a haughty spirit before a fall." My battles were not just about writing; they were also about not believing I had the right to assist other writers. I often thought, "Who am I? I am a nobody in the world of writing." However, God calls us to be humble and to serve others, as mentioned in Philippians 2:3: "Do nothing out of selfish ambition or vain conceit. Rather, in humility value others above yourselves." Therefore, let's remind ourselves that our worth is not measured by our achievements but by our willingness to help one another.

THE REALITY OF OBEDIENCE

Starting the journey of obedience can often feel like walking up a steep hill, difficult and exhausting. Many writers I've met did not begin with the intention of serving God through their words. Instead, they viewed writing as an obstacle, taking precious time away from their personal goals and dreams. But once they committed to the calling, they discovered unexpected joy and fulfillment. This made me think about how something that initially feels like a struggle can eventually become a blessing. Writing can be compared to a bridge: heavy and daunting at the start but ultimately leading us to blessings we didn't even know were awaiting us. To unlock these treasures, we first must surrender our lives to God.

Being a Kingdom Writer requires us to let go of our plans and embrace what God desires for us. This often means abandoning our own understanding and allowing the Holy Spirit to guide us. Instead of focusing on our desires, we focus on what God wants us to accomplish. This journey takes faith and trust, and it's important to remember that obedience is not about perfection; it's about working alongside God to create something beautiful, using the words that flow from our hearts.

Now, it's essential to clarify what obedience really means. It's not just a list of tasks we check off so we can feel worthy of God's love. The Bible teaches us in Romans 6:23, "For the wages of sin is death, but the free gift of God is eternal life through Christ Jesus our Lord." We can't earn our way into God's heart with good deeds; His love is a free gift given to us. Paul reminds us in Galatians 6:7-8 that our actions have consequences. If we live solely for ourselves, we risk facing decay and emptiness. However, if we choose to live by the Spirit, we open the door to everlasting life and joy.

True obedience stems from our faith in God's promises. It is in this belief that we find the strength and motivation to do good for others. Through our obedience, we produce "fruit" that brings glory to God and serves those around us. This means that our writing, inspired by God, can impact lives in ways we cannot even imagine. Each written word has the potential to touch hearts, inspire hope, and share the love of Christ with the world. As we embrace our roles as Kingdom Writers, let's remember the importance of trust in God. It is through this trust that we find the courage to step out in obedience, knowing that God has a unique plan for each of us. The path may not always be easy, but the blessings waiting at the end of our journey are worth every step we take in faith. Let us keep writing, trusting that God's light will guide us as we honor His call on our lives.

THE JOURNEY OF SACRIFICE

For many Kingdom Writers, the path to fulfilling their calling often requires a significant sacrifice, setting aside personal plans and desires in order to embrace the divine purpose that God has laid out for them. Now, this isn't always an easy journey! In fact, it can be rather uncomfortable. It might involve leaving behind the comfort of what you know. You may find yourself moving to new places, trying new things, and operating from a place of weakness in a world that values personal strength. Sometimes, we must admit that we have to let go of our established identities that took years to build. This can feel painful but remember John 15:2, "My Father examines every branch in Me and cuts away those who do not bear fruit. He leaves those bearing fruit and carefully prunes them so that they will bear more fruit." This pruning, while challenging, is essential for our growth.

As Kingdom Writers, it's vital to turn to God, our ultimate guide and the Great Author of our lives. We need to trust that He will lead and direct us in our writing. It's important to recognize that all writers have a responsibility to seek God actively and believe wholeheartedly in His role as the creator of their stories. In 2 Corinthians 12:8-9, Paul shares his experience of weakness and dependence on God: "My grace is all you need. My power works best in weakness." When we approach our writing from a place of humility and reliance on God's strength, we allow His grace to flow through us, transforming our weaknesses into powerful messages.

However, the enemy can subtly distract us, leading us to focus on our own desires rather than God's calling. If he can tempt us into prioritizing our comfort, he can hinder our ability to write and share the messages that need to be delivered. It can be so easy to unwind after a long day, choosing to indulge in a repetitive routine, while deep inside, there's a whisper urging you to turn off the distractions and get to work. I know this struggle all too well. While creating this collection of books, I faced the same temptations (this will be further explored in my companion book, *Testimony of a Kingdom Writer*), often without realizing I was succumbing to the enemy's agenda instead of God's.

It's crucial to understand that not having a lot, be it time, money, or resources, is not an excuse to hold back your gifts. Why? Because your gift is where your abundance is found. While there is a balance between being responsible and sacrificing, we must bring our best to God and trust that He will provide for our needs. Our heart posture shouldn't be, "I'll write for God if He gives me something in return," but rather, our actions should stem from genuine faith and obedience to His call. Remember, everything we possess ultimately belongs to God. For every Kingdom Writer, there's an undeniable truth: operating in your divine purpose will come at a cost. We may face difficult times, but we must not falter, for these tribulations serve to bring glory to

God. Keep in mind that God is always with us, ensuring we are supported throughout our journey.

Just like Abraham, who left his familiar life behind to follow God's call, we too may be asked to step out of our comfort zones and face new challenges in order to achieve our writing dreams. As Hebrews 11:8 (NIV) reminds us, "By faith Abraham, when called to go to a place he would later receive as his inheritance, obeyed and went, even though he did not know where he was going." This example shows us that stepping out in faith can lead us to incredible opportunities and blessings, even when the path ahead is uncertain. For you, this journey may come with pressures and uncertainties, but as Luke 12:48 teaches, "But someone who does not know, and then does something wrong, will be punished only lightly. When someone has been given much, much will be required in return; and when someone has been entrusted with much, even more will be required." God's work often calls us to leave our cozy bubbles and embrace the unknown, trusting that He will guide and provide. If we choose to neglect our calling, we risk hindering the growth and encouragement that the body of Christ desperately needs from our unique gifts and stories. Even as we courageously follow where God leads, it's important to remain mindful of the temptations and comforts that can so easily distract us from our true purpose, remembering always that God equips us for every step of the journey.

Distractions of comfort will undoubtedly come, but we don't have to answer the door when they knock. God has already designed a plan for us, and getting ahead of it can open the door to confusion and doubt. God paid a hefty price with His only Son to reconcile us and set us on the right path. Our desires should align with God's will.

Take a moment to reflect:

Are you using your time effectively when you feel God calling you to write? Are there distractions preventing you from accomplishing His purpose? If God were to inquire today about what you have written so far for Him, how would you respond?

As Kingdom Writers, our mission is to deliver our message in a timely and effective manner, which often requires sacrificing our immediate desires for God's greater plan. Moreover, it's essential to surround ourselves with people who encourage and uplift our spiritual journey. Friends who share your faith can provide the guidance and prayer support needed when challenges arise. For instance, when you feel overwhelmed and think about quitting, listen to those friends who encourage you to stay the course. They can help you remember your call to write is bigger than you. Those aligned with you spiritually understand the significance of your mission and won't let you falter in your purpose. On the flip side, those who don't share your walk with Christ might unintentionally steer you away from your calling, suggesting excuses that serve the enemy's agenda.

Remember that Kingdom Writers aren't swayed by the praise or compliments of others; instead, we listen and obey the call we have received. We are planting seeds through our words, even if we may not witness the fruit of our labor in this lifetime. Our calling may have a specific audience, but the beauty of our God-given purpose is that we don't get to choose where it leads us. Our mission is to go wherever God calls us and write whatever He puts on our hearts. As you study God's Word, ensure your writing reflects His truth and is presented simply for others to understand. Remember, sacrifice is a part of the journey, but with God on our side, we can fulfill our purpose and inspire others in the process.

PRIDE & HUMILITY

As we start to explore the concepts of pride and humility, it's crucial to understand that humility is the core of a Kingdom Writer's mission. Humility doesn't mean viewing ourselves as less important; instead, it's about acknowledging who we really are in God's sight. The Bible tells us, "I am what I am by the grace of God" (1 Corinthians 15:10). This grace provides us with all we need to fulfill our calling. A true Kingdom Writer understands that their talent for writing comes from God, not from themselves. When we accept this reality, it opens doors to opportunities greater than we can imagine. By embracing our identity and the gifts we've received, we can pursue our God-given purpose without being weighed down by unnecessary pride.

Pride can lead us down a harmful path, similar to the cities of Sodom and Gomorrah, which fell because they turned away from God's truth. When we choose pride over humility, we risk facing serious consequences. However, in humility, we find hope. The Bible teaches that when we humble ourselves, God will lift us up (James 4:10). This is especially important for Kingdom Writers. The stories we create can soar to heights we cannot reach alone; it is God who guides us and elevates our work. Our moments of shame and struggle can transform into powerful stories of hope when we lean into God's grace and let Him reshape our writing.

Another challenge writers face is self-centeredness. Have you ever seen another author's work and felt discouraged, questioning, "Why should I write when their book is similar?" This thought reveals a focus on self-centeredness instead of the message. It is vital to remember that writing is not just for our benefit, it aims to touch others. Every writer has a unique voice and a specific audience, and that voice is meant to touch, influence, and inspire the very people they are called to reach. Your writing carries the power to make a meaningful difference in the lives of your audience, connecting with them in ways only you can. When another author achieves success, it doesn't diminish your calling; instead, it creates chances for collaboration and mutual growth. God wants us to support one another on this journey because our mission is far greater than individual success. Embracing our roles as writers means understanding we are part of something larger. Just as Jesus said in John 14:12, "Anyone who believes in me will do the same works I have done, and even greater works," we too have a purpose that goes beyond ourselves. Each word we write can move hearts and inspire change. Our writing should not be self-serving; it should connect with the needs of those around us. When we grasp this truth, we can shift our attention from prideful comparisons to the joy of serving others through our words. Let our writing be a means for God to reach out, offer encouragement, and uplift those who read our work.

On this journey, let us continually seek humility, understanding that our abilities as Kingdom Writers come from God alone. As we humble ourselves, we will witness amazing changes—not just in our own lives, but also in the lives of those we impact with our stories. By offering grace to ourselves and to others, we can create a supportive community of writers who both encourage and inspire us. Let this be our mission: to write with purpose and passion, to find encouragement in one another, and to remember that our calling is never just for our own benefit. We are vessels meant to share God's love and truth, bringing hope and inspiration to those who read our work. Together, we can fulfill the amazing potential God has placed within us as we humble ourselves before Him and boldly step into our writing journey.

UNDERSTANDING THE POWER OF PRAYER

Prayer is an intimate talk with God, rooted in our understanding of His love for us. As Ephesians 1:18 tells us, we should pray for understanding, giving us hope in our calling as writers. We must pour out our hearts and trust that God will fill us with fresh ideas and inspiration every day. Even when we feel overwhelmed, like after a busy day or a tough writing session, we can ask God for help and look to Him for clarity and abundance. Writing then turns into a ministry, a way to shine light on the hope and life we find in Christ to others. Prayer is a wonderful gift that helps us connect deeply and personally with God. My understanding of prayer changed a lot after my mother passed away. This great loss made me realize how much I had taken for granted by not consistently praying. I shared my feelings with my husband, wondering what might improve in my life if I committed to praying every day. I knew God listened to our prayers, and I realized my life was about to gain new meaning, especially in learning how to find peace during the many changes of life. Losing my mother was a significant moment; I understood that although my life would never be the same, moving forward with God was my only choice, and that thought encouraged me.

So, I decided to dedicate three special moments each day to prayer. In the morning, right after waking, I express my gratitude to God. This helps me acknowledge that God gives me another day of life, especially after remembering how fragile life can be. I thank God for His patience, His forgiveness, and the amazing gift of Jesus, who sacrificed Himself for us. Through Jesus, I am made whole again, and recognizing this transformation is an essential part of my daily gratitude. I also thank God for my mother, who showed me faith and love, guiding me toward my purpose and helping me understand how to live according to His Word.

During my afternoon prayer, I share my requests with God while also thanking Him for His will in my life. As a writer, I often feel unsure about my path and sometimes inadequate. With having a PhD, I often find myself presented with incredible job opportunities that come with excellent benefits and high pay; however, these roles do not align with my true calling and tend to hinder or completely halt my writing. I frequently struggle with the dilemma of whether to accept these positions and transform my family's life or to remain faithful to my writing as a commitment to God. Thankfully, my husband encourages me to pause, take a step back, and remember to focus on writing, reminding me to follow the path God has laid out for me because I have work to do. Ultimately, I realized he was right in trusting that God's plan empowers me to continue pursuing my divine call. So, I pray for the strength to concentrate on writing what God desires, rather than getting caught up in distractions or concerns about provision. I also remember my family and friends during this time, asking God to fulfill the desires of their heart's according to His will, knowing He hears every request. This prayer time also reminds me that many people are hurting and lost, and I lift them up, asking God to guide them toward His light.

As the day ends, my evening prayer becomes a time for reflection. I look back on the day's events with God, recognizing where I felt His guidance and where I may have stumbled. That day was filled with both challenges and blessings. I am thankful for each writing opportunity and the gentle nudges from the Holy Spirit that push me to use my time wisely. There is something profound about using both the good and chaotic moments of life to help others find God. Recently, I had the chance to pray for someone in need and realizing that God had answered their prayer strengthened my desire to be obedient in praying for others.

Prayer is more than just sharing our wishes; it's about trusting fully in who God is and what He can do with our lives when we believe in Him. I discovered comforting verses like Malachi 3:6, which reminds us that God does not change, providing reassurance in tough times. Every Scripture I read motivates me and strengthens my writing. I realize how important it is to set aside time each day, not just to read His Word, but to pray and talk to God, allowing Him to help me understand His plans, bridging the gap between my doubts and the confidence I need to follow my calling. God has a unique purpose for each of us, and through prayer and study, we can discover that purpose. As we embark on this writing journey, let us remember that God shows no favoritism. Each one of us is cherished equally in His sight. Imagine a world where we all used our talents to uplift one another, there would be no need left unmet!

In our journey as writers, embracing prayer is essential, and one beautiful way to pray is by speaking in tongues. This special gift is available to all believers and can significantly enhance our writing. When we communicate with God in our heavenly language, as mentioned in 1 Corinthians 14:2, we deepen and strengthen our connection to His divine purpose for us as writers. Although our time on earth is limited, we have countless opportunities to share God's goodness through our words. Each day, I pray for all writers: may we rise with enthusiasm to express our thoughts, inspired by the Holy Spirit. Remember, our words are not just for us; they are meant to glorify God and spread His love throughout the world. Let us always listen for His guidance as we embark on our unique writing paths, fully trusting in His perfect plan for our lives.

UNDERSTANDING FASTING

If you're anything like me, the idea of fasting might initially feel daunting and overwhelming. When I first heard the term *fasting*, I thought, "No way!" I was the person who believed that praying was sufficient and that fasting was meant for those who were super spiritual. I first attempted it when I was in my thirties, and let me tell you, I was a bundle of nerves. I decided to fast just for lunch, but I remember waking up that day with a massive breakfast and stressing myself out in anticipation. At around 11:45 a.m., the panic set in. My mind was racing, telling me I was starving despite having just eaten a big meal and boy did I complain to everyone. I was left confused and anxious rather than focused on seeking God.

That experience, along with a few others, taught me that I was missing the point of fasting, it wasn't about food, but about spiritual growth. As stated in Matthew 6:16-18, Jesus teaches us, "And when you fast, don't make it obvious, as the hypocrites do, for they try to look miserable and disheveled so people will admire them for their fasting. I tell you the truth, that is the only reward they will ever get. But when you fast, comb your hair and wash your face. Then no one will notice that you are fasting, except your Father, who knows what you do in private. And your Father, who sees everything, will reward you." These verses emphasize that the purpose of fasting is not to show off but to deepen our relationship with God.

Many people might feel a similar hesitation as I did about fasting. Some may have never tried it and feel afraid to admit that. Others may have tried and felt like they failed, leading them to shy away from fasting altogether. Then there are those who fast but aren't always content with what God reveals to them, perhaps even fearing a call that deviates from their personal desires. Yet, there are also individuals who embrace fasting joyfully, receiving clear guidance from God, and readily obeying His will. To those of you who are finding success in your fasting journey, I am genuinely inspired by your dedication. I aspire to grow and learn how to submit to God's will as you do. My own journey with fasting has been a gradual and rewarding process, one that has evolved significantly over time.

Fasting has played a significant role in my life, especially after I turned forty. (I must admit, I didn't fully embrace it until then, so please don't judge!) Like many others, I always thought that not eating would not help me hear God's voice. After all, isn't God a good God? I wondered how enjoying a tasty cheeseburger and fries could affect my connection with Him. In fact, I often felt I could hear Him better when my stomach wasn't screaming like a toddler for my attention. Yet, life has its own way of steering us toward growth. I began to feel a strong desire to learn about fasting, inspired by my mother, who often prayed and fasted. It dawned on me that fasting wasn't just for a select few; it was an opportunity I could also explore for my own benefit. If my mother could do it, why couldn't I?

As writers, taking the time to fast can help clear our minds and sharpen our focus, leading us to better understand ourselves and the messages we wish to convey. Fasting can be a powerful tool for writers, especially when seeking clarity and direction in our work. I began my fasting journey not just for myself, but for my transportation and logistics business. As a business owner, I chose to fast twice a year, dedicating myself to this spiritual practice. The first fast was a three-week (21day) commitment at the beginning of the year. During this time, I earnestly sought God's guidance for my trucking business, aiming to align my choices with His will instead of chasing my desires. I even invited my staff to be part of this prayer and fasting experience. It was important that we refrain from making any major decisions during this period, even when faced with tempting offers that seemingly came out of nowhere. I remembered the teachings from the Bible, such as Proverbs 3:5-6, which says, "Trust in the Lord with all your heart and lean not on your own understanding; in all your ways submit to Him, and He will make your paths straight." This reminded me to remain obedient and patient, trusting that God had brought us to this point for a reason. In September, I would also undertake a week-long fast, focusing on praying for direction and clarity in my personal life. This practice proved vital, as it became a time for reflection and honing my understanding of what God wanted for me.

Nowadays, as a writer, my prayer and fasting has shifted in purpose. At the start of every year, I commit to a three-week fast, dedicating this time to seek God about my call as a Kingdom Writer and what paths He desires for me to take when it comes to getting the finished book into the hands of those, He wants to read it. For example, I use this time to ask God to guide me on whether I should publish my work independently or pursue a traditional publisher. If it's meant for me to self-publish, I fast and pray that God will lead the right team members to me, colleagues He wants in my corner, people who will help me fulfill His purpose. If I'm not meant to publish on my own, I fast and pray that God will continue to order the steps of the publishing team I'll need, making sure that everyone involved is aligned with His will. There are also areas in my writing journey where I experience uncertainty, particularly in marketing. Despite being a business professor, promoting myself doesn't come easily, likely due to my own insecurities in the past. Therefore, during these fasting periods, I also ask God to take the lead, especially in aspects where I feel weak.

In September, I become even more intentional about my role as a writer, spending extra time in prayer for clarity and direction—not only for the audiences I serve, but also for any unexpected distractions that could slow my progress. I also turn my attention inward, focusing more on my personal life and asking, "What does God want me to focus on right now, and why?" Any questions or uncertainties that arise during this season, I bring before God, trusting Him to provide the answers and guidance I need. Overall fasting has become an essential part of understanding and embracing my calling, and I'd love to extend that invitation to you. I sincerely encourage you to consider embarking on your own fasting journey, even if it means starting small. You don't have to jump into a three-week (21day) fast right away. Start with just one meal. Or if you find yourself caught up in social media, perhaps consider fasting from it during your time with God. Avoid the temptation of filling that time with other distractions. Instead, dedicate that time solely to the Lord, without interference. I am confident that by creating this space for prayer and reflection, you will not only deepen your relationship with God but also enhance your writing. Remember, fasting is not just about giving up food; it's about strengthening your spiritual connection and gaining clarity by removing the distractions that keep you from hearing God clearly.

DISCIPLESHIP

As Kingdom Writers, we have an important job: Our mission is to bring the principles and truths of heaven to earth through our writing.

This mission is essential, and the Bible guides us in understanding its importance. In Matthew 28:19-20, Jesus tells us, "Go therefore and make disciples of all nations, baptizing them in the name of the Father and of the Son and of the Holy Spirit." This call to action reminds us that we are more than just storytellers; we are like lighthouses in a world that can often seem dark and confusing. God promises to be with us always, which gives us the courage to share our unique messages with confidence. We are not just writers; we are pioneers on a journey that others can follow to discover their purpose.

Writing should not be about seeking fame or recognition. Instead, it stems from our own life experiences and testimonies. Each of us has a story that plays a part in expanding God's Kingdom. Think about this: What if someone secretly reads your book and finds the hope they have been looking for? This thought should motivate every writer, reminding us of the power of expressing ourselves in obedience to God. Our writing can serve as a form of discipleship, speaking to the hearts of those who are seeking, and showing that great things can come from humble beginnings. In these moments, we realize our writing carries purpose and offers God a chance to work through us.

As writers, we are natural missionaries called to help grow God's Kingdom. After we dedicate our lives to Christ, we become part of His loving plan to help save others. The goal of our writing is to reach those who are lost and guide them to a relationship with Jesus. Every person we meet who does not know Christ is a mission opportunity, and each word we write can illuminate the one and only pathway to salvation. This perspective has changed how I view my writing and its potential. What if my stories lead someone, maybe a friend or family member, to experience the beautiful love of Jesus? This realization inspires me to write with purpose, knowing my obedience has unlimited potential to ignite faith in others. Embracing this calling, we recognize that our words can do more than inform, they can disciple, encourage, and lead others closer to Christ.

Discipleship through writing is not only about telling a great story, but about sharing what we believe in our hearts. Every writer's journey is different, but our shared goal is to lead others to Christ. As Kingdom Writers, we strive to live out this teaching through our work, allowing our words to motivate and challenge others to grow in their faith. By sharing our personal beliefs and life experiences, we invite readers to start their own spiritual journeys and encourage them to stay strong in their walk with God.

When we write with authenticity and vulnerability, we create a safe space for others to see themselves in our stories and to recognize God's hand at work in their own lives. Our testimonies, both the victories and the struggles, become powerful reminders that no one is alone in their faith journey. Through our writing, we can address doubts, offer hope in seasons of waiting, and remind others that God's promises are true for everyone. In this way, our words serve as both a light and a guide, pointing readers back to the source of all wisdom and comfort. As we continue to write, let us remember that our obedience and willingness to share our hearts can plant seeds of faith that God will nurture in His perfect timing.

To fully embrace our calling as writers, we also must stay aware of the different seasons in our lives. Understanding that everyone's journey is unique helps us appreciate the individuality of each person's path. Not everyone will understand us or travel alongside us, and that is perfectly okay. What's most important is that we are faithfully following the path God has set out for us. This sensitivity lets us write from a place of honesty, which resonates with those who read our work. By sharing our stories, we foster a supportive community and promote discipleship in many forms. In this wonderful process, we hold the power to inspire change and growth in ourselves and in our readers, truly embodying what it means to be Kingdom Writers.

———

CHAPTER 5 SUMMARY: OUR RESPONSIBILITY AS WRITERS

In this chapter, we explore the responsibility that comes with being a Kingdom Writer. Writing is not merely an act of creativity, but a calling to share God's truth and light with the world. The chapter emphasizes the importance of understanding our divine purpose and seeking

God's guidance throughout our writing journey. We are reminded to reflect on how our words can lead others to Christ.

The chapter also discusses the need for thoughtful balance in our writing, recognizing when to listen versus when to share. We must resist the urge to compare ourselves and acknowledge ourselves as unique creations of God, embracing our individuality. Additionally, we explore the significance of staying rooted in the Bible, allowing God's Word to inspire and shape our writing. It emphasizes the transformative power of prayer and meditation, as well as how fasting can enhance our spiritual clarity.

Furthermore, the chapter reinforces the importance of obedience to God's call and remaining humble throughout our writing processes. Sacrifice is highlighted as an essential aspect of fulfilling our writing journey, requiring us to let go of personal desires for God's greater purpose. Lastly, the call to discipleship through writing echoes prominently, reminding us that our mission transcends personal achievement, urging us to uplift and guide others in their faith.

ACTION STEPS

1. **Reflect on Purpose:** Take time to contemplate your role as a writer. Ask yourself how your words can lead others to Christ.
2. **Seek Guidance:** Spend regular moments in prayer and meditation to quiet distractions and listen for God's voice.
3. **Embrace Individuality:** Celebrate your unique writing style and resist the urge to compare yourself to other writers. Affirm your identity as a child of God.
4. **Engage with Scriptures:** Dedicate time daily to read and meditate on the Bible. Let Scripture inform your writing and inspire your messages.
5. **Practice Fasting:** Consider fasting from distractions, such as food or social media, to enhance your focus on God and seek clarity in your writing journey.
6. **Commit to Obedience:** Write with a spirit of obedience,

always aligning your work with God's purpose rather than your ambitions.

7. **Encourage Discipleship:** Write with the intention of guiding others closer to God, sharing your personal insights and experiences to uplift and inspire.

8. **Build Community:** Surround yourself with fellow writers who share your faith, offering and receiving support on your shared journey.

Through these actionable steps, you can honor your calling as a Kingdom Writer, carrying out your unique mission to inspire and encourage others through the words you write.

CHAPTER 6
Your Greatest Decision

LET ME TAKE A MOMENT to share something truly important with you. This chapter is the most significant and the hardest one for me to write. It serves as an invitation for you to take your very first step toward a new life by giving your heart to Christ. I spent a lot of time pondering how to convey this message, seeking God's guidance on what to say. What I realized is that I don't want you to merely recite the prayer of salvation without truly understanding its meaning. Anyone can say, "Jesus is Lord," but we must avoid what I call the "parrot effect," where words are repeated without genuine understanding. I've always felt that a relationship should be authentic and meaningful. Therefore, I need to share the full picture with you. To begin, let's talk about some of the incredible gifts of mercy (in no particular order) that God bestows upon us when we give our lives to Christ. These gifts create a solid foundation for understanding why giving your life to Christ isn't merely a ritual, but a profound transformation. To help you truly grasp the significance of this step, let's begin by looking at some of the remarkable gifts God offers to those who accept Him.

First is the gift of knowledge, which is found in the teachings of the Bible. The Word of God acts as a guiding light in our lives, illuminating our paths in a world that can sometimes feel dark and confusing. Romans 1:16-17 says, "For I am not ashamed of this Good News about Christ. It is the power of God at work, saving everyone who believes." This truth reminds us that faith is essential to being reconciled with God. It's amazing to think that through faith, we begin a new journey as part of His family. Beyond illuminating our path with knowledge, God graciously grants us the time and patience needed to walk that path at our own pace.

Another remarkable gift is the gift of time and God's patience toward us. I must admit how grateful I am for this gift! If God had not given me the time to repent and get my life back on track, I may not have been able to share these words with you today. I have faced struggles in various aspects of life, particularly with writing and sharing my thoughts. The fact that God has allowed me time to grow and learn demonstrates His immense love and care. Romans 2:3-4 reminds us of His kindness, encouraging us to turn away from our wrongdoings. His patience is a beautiful expression of His desire for us to choose the right path, which is the one that leads us closer to Him.

Next is the beautiful gift of redemption, which was purchased at a high price: the life of Jesus Christ. This sacrifice is something no one else could match or even fathom. Redemption means we are rescued and freed from the bondage of sin, a powerful act of God's love. Romans 3:24 states, "Yet God, in his grace, freely makes us right in his sight. He did this through Christ Jesus when he freed us from the penalty for our sins." Through Christ's sacrifice, we are granted freedom from the bondage of sin. Understanding this gift is crucial because it tells us how deeply God cares for us, for He paid the ultimate price to bring us back into a loving relationship with Him.

Continuing our journey, we see the gift of remission. Through Jesus's death on the cross, we are released from the penalties of sin. "Remission" means to be discharged and set free. Romans 3:25 highlights this, assuring us that we are made right with God through faith in Jesus's sacrifice. This gift is a beautiful reminder of God's endless grace and how He chooses to pardon us, letting go of our past wrongs. This grace is offered to all who believe, making it clear that God desires to have a relationship with each of us, no matter our past.

The next incredible gift is that of justification. This gift means that once you sincerely say the salvation prayer and conclude with "Amen," God considers you righteous. Your identity changes forever, and no one can take that away from you. Justification happens the moment you accept Christ, marking you as part of God's family. Justification isn't dependent on how we feel, but rooted in the truth that God promises. Romans 3:24 reminds us of this: "Yet God, in his grace, freely makes us right in his sight."

Justification refers to God perceiving you as if you have never sinned. However, this does not mean that you can act recklessly without consequence. There is still important work to be done to reach this state, known as sanctification. Justification serves as a label for your life. Sanctification, which is a lifelong journey, involves striving to do the right thing each day, step by step, from the moment you are born again until you see Jesus face to face. In essence, justification is an act initiated by God, while sanctification is humanity's response to that divine act. The gift of justification is remarkable because it is not based on your actions but rather on your faith in Jesus Christ. It is a declaration, not an accomplishment. Understanding how God views you will guide how you should live, and your behavior should reflect how God sees you.

As we delve deeper into God's mercies, another gift we receive is freedom from the penalty and power of sin. This is a powerful truth! The enemy wants to keep you unaware of your freedom, but you can walk in a new life, free from the control of sin. Romans 6:4 teaches us that, through Christ, we can live a new life. When we commit ourselves to Him, we are no longer slaves to sin, but we are empowered to live according to God's calling. Understanding this freedom allows us to renew our minds daily through the Word, embrace the new identity God offers us, and transform our lives to live with purpose.

Finally, we arrive at the gifts of no condemnation and the presence of the Holy Spirit. Romans 8:1 reassures us that there is no condemnation for those who belong to Christ Jesus, such powerful words of hope! You are not living under a life sentence of separation from God. Furthermore, you are never alone. The Holy Spirit is your helper and comforter, guiding you through life's challenges. Romans 8:11-13 explains this miraculous gift: "The Spirit of God, who raised Jesus from the dead, lives in you. And just as God raised Christ Jesus from the dead, he will give life to your mortal bodies by this same Spirit living within you. Therefore, dear brothers and sisters, you have no obligation to do what your sinful nature urges you to do. For if you live by its dictates, you will die. But if through the power of the Spirit you put to death the deeds of your sinful nature, you will live" This profound truth means that we can find strength and guidance daily. So, dear friend, after seeing just a small glimpse of the many gifts you will receive from God, I invite you to make the most important decision you will ever make: to accept Jesus Christ into your life as your Lord and Savior. The journey ahead is one filled with purpose, love, and immense joy!

I WANT A RELATIONSHIP WITH GOD

Have you ever felt the beauty of nature around you, the vibrant colors of the sky, the gentle rustling of the leaves, or the magnificent mountains? Romans 1:20 tells us that since the world was created, people can see God's incredible qualities through everything He made. It's like nature is whispering to us about His eternal power and divine nature, leaving us without an excuse for not knowing Him. If you're reading this and don't have a relationship with God just yet, that's okay! Today could be your special day to start this beautiful journey. It's entirely normal to feel a bit lost when you encounter Scripture if you haven't experienced God personally before, but don't let that discourage you. There's something deep within you that keeps pulling you back to this message. And that very desire is God's calling, inviting you to continue reading and exploring His Word.

As we embark on this journey together, I want to encourage you to prioritize reading the Bible above all else, even above this book. While this is an introductory book meant to help guide and support you as a Kingdom writer, always remember that the most important book you can ever read and the one that will always remain the most important, is the Bible. My hope is that you allow God's Word to fill your heart at least three times more than anything you take in from these pages. Remember, every time you spend time in the Bible, you're strengthening your relationship with God, uncovering more about your true identity, and gaining clearer insight into your unique calling. If you ever feel overwhelmed by your call to be a Kingdom writer, know that you're not alone. No matter where you are on your writing journey, trust that every moment you invest in God's Word will produce lasting fruit in your spirit.

UNDERSTANDING THE PRAYER OF SALVATION

It's important to understand that the enemy doesn't want you to pave this path toward a relationship with Christ. He may whisper doubts in your ear, telling you that you're not ready or that you need to fix yourself first. I've been there, and let me tell you, these are lies meant to hold you back. The truth is that all of us have sinned and fall short of the glory of God (Romans 3:23). It doesn't matter who we are or what we've done, we are all equal in our need for God's love. When I realized that I don't have to earn God's love, everything changed. This is where Grace becomes essential. It's about God's unearned favor being given freely to us. Embracing your relationship with Jesus means freedom from your past and opening new doors to a brighter future.

Having a relationship with Christ significantly impacts your life, guiding you through challenges and struggles. It's not just about spending eternity with God; it's about understanding His deep love for you right now. As you walk with Him, you will begin to uncover who you truly are in Him. Your identity matters, and it's directly linked to your purpose and calling. Discovering your role as a writer for God's Kingdom means knowing and embracing your identity in Him. This is essential; without that understanding, you might feel uncertain about your contribution to the world around you. So, if you're longing to know Jesus and connect with Him, I would like to invite you to take the first step through a simple prayer.

Understanding the prayer of salvation is a beautiful journey that begins with recognizing our need for God. Every single person makes mistakes and faces challenges. We all miss the mark, and that's okay!

It's a part of being human. The first part of the prayer is when we realize we need help and turn our hearts toward God, we take the first step toward forgiveness and a fresh start. Remember that acknowledging our faults is not a reason to feel shame, but a doorway to achieving a deeper and loving relationship with our Creator.

The middle section of the prayer reminds us of how deeply God cares for us: "But God demonstrates his own love for us in this: While we were still sinners, Christ died for us" (Romans 5:8). This is such a powerful statement! It shows that God loved us even when we were not perfect. Imagine that! Even before we knew Him or thought of turning our lives around, He made the ultimate sacrifice out of love. This love is like a warm embrace, welcoming us back home into His arms. Every time we pray and express our desire for a closer relationship with Him, we remind ourselves of this incredible fact. It's like telling God, "I believe in Your love for me!"

As we reach the end of the prayer, we find the promise of salvation: "For everyone who calls on the name of the Lord will be saved" (Romans 10:13). This means that if we sincerely reach out to God and ask for His help, He is there. This is a wonderful promise for everyone, no matter where they are on their journey. Just imagine, at that moment, when you call out to God and ask Him to be part of your life, you are not alone. You are creating a forever connection. It's like opening a door to a new adventure, one filled with grace, mercy, and endless love from above.

Let's take a moment to pray a prayer together, known as the prayer of salvation. This is the beginning of seeking God, discovering His immense love for you, recognizing your identity, and understanding your unique purpose. If you can, please join me in this prayer. Embrace this moment as a beautiful opportunity to open your heart, to take that first step into a wondrous relationship that will forever transform your life.

Father, in the name of Jesus,

I admit that I am a sinner and have done many things that don't please you. I have lived my life for myself only. I am sorry, and I repent. I ask you to forgive me.

I believe that you lived and died on the cross for me, to save me. You did what I could not do for myself. I come to you now and ask you to take control of my life; I give it to you. From this day forward, help me to live every day for you, and in a way that pleases you. Right now, I confess Jesus as my Lord. With my whole heart, I believe God raised Jesus from the grave. I accept Jesus Christ as my personal Savior, and according to His Word, I am saved.

In Jesus' name, I pray. Amen.

I want to take a moment to applaud you for saying this prayer and taking steps toward a deeper connection with God. It's no small feat, and I am incredibly proud of you! This budding relationship is just the beginning of something beautiful. Keep in mind that spending time in the Bible helps us stay focused and understand God's Word better. Writing down what you read can help you remember it and come back to it whenever you need encouragement or guidance. Think of it as gathering treasures to keep in your heart. With time, as you continue this practice, God will reveal more of His wisdom and love to you.

Oh, and let me share some exciting news! Right now, there's a whole host of angels celebrating your decision to seek a relationship with God. In Luke 15:10, it says, "In the same way, there is joy in the presence of God's angels when even one sinner repents." Isn't that wonderful? You are not just starting a personal journey, but you're joining a joyful celebration in heaven! Each decision you make to follow God brings happiness not only to you but also to the heavenly hosts. Hold on to that joy and let it inspire you to grow in your faith.

As you move forward, remember that following Jesus is a journey, and it's okay to take baby steps along the way. One key insight I wish someone had shared with me is that we don't need to improve ourselves to start following Christ. Instead, it's about allowing Jesus to help us grow. Some days will be easier than others, and that's perfectly normal. Don't be hard on yourself if you stumble; everyone does at times, including me. The important part is repenting and learning from those moments, not getting stuck in feelings of failure. Your identity in Christ is solid, and you have a new label: justified! So, breathe in that lovely new identity. You are forgiven, loved, and accepted. Celebrate the wonderful journey ahead and cherish the knowledge that you are not alone. With each prayer, each verse learned, and every step taken in faith, you are growing closer to God. Let that warm feeling fill your heart, knowing that you are part of His family, now and forever!

PRAYER OF RECOMMITMENT

Some of you may have already committed your life to Christ, but you might feel that your relationship with God is not where you want it to be. When we find ourselves distanced from God, it can be a challenging and lonely place to be. Many of us have walked that path, feeling as though we are too far gone to return. I want to encourage you today: you are never beyond God's reach! No matter how many times life tries to pull you away from your relationship with Him, you have the power to take a step back into His loving embrace. Today marks a new beginning, a recommitment not just in words, but in heart and spirit, reaffirming your desire to stay close to God regardless of what challenges lay ahead.

Remember, God is always ready to welcome you back with open arms. As we prepare to pray together, it's important to understand the significance of a prayer of recommitment. This is not merely a matter of repeating words; it is about purposeful communication with God. Through this prayer, you express your intention to turn away from sin and turn back to Christ. Repentance is a heartfelt decision that requires sincerity and determination. By acknowledging our weaknesses and seeking God's strength, we begin to pave the way for His love and grace to fill our lives. In the Bible, Acts 3:19 reminds us, "Repent, then, and turn to God, so that your sins may be wiped out," emphasizing the transformative power of true repentance.

When we pray, I want you to focus on four key elements that make our prayer meaningful. The first element is thankfulness. We show our gratitude to God for His unwavering forgiveness and His support as we strive to become more like Him. Second, take a moment to think about the sins you wrestle with. Being specific allows you to lay them out before God honestly. Our third point highlights an essential truth:

we cannot overcome sin by ourselves. On our own, we are weak, but with God's help, we can rise above it. Finally, we must trust that God hears our prayers always. He has gifted us the Holy Spirit, which guides us as we navigate life's challenges, reminding us that we are not fighting sin alone.

As we look forward to saying this prayer together, let's remember the foundation of our faith. Jesus, who died and rose again, is alive today and sits beside the Father, interceding for us. Sin has no power over you when you declare the name of Jesus, and every knee will bow to His authority. We can confidently claim our freedom from sin and the burdens that can weigh us down and distract us from our purpose. Today, let's break those chains together, allowing God's power to lift us and guide us back toward our calling in life.

So, if you're ready, I invite you to join me in this prayer of recommitment. By doing so, you are taking an important step towards rededicating your life to Him. You'll rediscover His love, recognize your true identity, and understand the purpose you hold in this world. Let us bow our heads and pray together.

> **Father, in the name of Jesus,**
>
> **I am not perfect. Create in me a pure heart, O God, and renew a steadfast spirit within me (Psalm 51:10). Thank you for being faithful to forgive my sins when I confess them to you. Thank you for the gift of repentance and forgiveness. Through the help of the Holy Spirit, I'm able to fight against sin. I pray that you help me turn away from the sins [list your sins] I'm struggling with. Forgive me for committing these sins. Today is the day that I will look back and say that my life got back on track and I began to operate fully in the middle of your will even when I did not realize it.**
>
> **In the mighty name of Jesus I pray. Amen.**

In this moment of renewed commitment, I want to take a moment to celebrate you! By engaging in this prayer, you've taken a significant step toward deepening your relationship with God, and that is something truly wonderful. This restored bond marks the beginning of an incredible journey. Remember, spending time in the Word is vital; it sharpens our focus and deepens our understanding of God. Consider journaling what resonates with you as you read these notes will serve as cherished reminders and sources of encouragement whenever you need them. Think of it as collecting treasures for your heart. With perseverance and faith, as you embrace this practice, God's wisdom and love will unfold in beautiful ways.

CHAPTER 6 SUMMARY: UNDERSTANDING GOD'S GIFTS OF MERCY

In this chapter, a heartfelt invitation is extended for everyone to either take their first step toward a new life by accepting Christ or making a recommitment to Him. It is important to genuinely understand what this relationship means, rather than just repeating a prayer without comprehension. This chapter emphasizes that various gifts of mercy are given by God when we open our hearts to Him, and these gifts lay the foundation for a meaningful connection.

KEY POINTS FROM THE CHAPTER

1. **Gift of Knowledge:** The teachings of the Bible guide us on our journey. Romans 1:16-17 tells us that faith in Christ is our way to be made right with God.

2. **Gift of Time & Patience:** We all need time to grow and learn. Romans 2:3-4 reminds us that God is kind and patient, encouraging us to turn from wrongdoings.

3. **Gift of Redemption:** Jesus' sacrifice freed us from sin. Romans 3:24 explains that through Him, we are rescued from sin's hold on us.

4. **Gift of Remission:** Through Jesus' death, we are forgiven and set free from sin's penalties. Romans 3:25 shows us that God pardons those who believe.

5. **Gift of Justification:** When we accept Christ, God sees us as righteous. Romans 3:24 assures us that we are made right in His sight, in spite of our past.

6. **Gift of Freedom:** Romans 6:4 tells us that through Christ, we can live a new life, free from the control of sin.

7. **Gift of No Condemnation:** Romans 8:1 states that there is no condemnation for those in Christ. We are not alone; the Holy Spirit guides us.

ACTION STEPS

1. **Accept Christ:** If you haven't already, consider praying to invite Jesus into your life or recommit to making Him your Lord and Savior.
2. **Read the Bible:** Spend time in God's Word. Let it guide your heart and thoughts more than anything else.
3. **Pray Regularly:** Talk to God daily. Use the prayer of salvation to open your heart and ask for guidance.
4. **Journal Your Journey:** Write down your thoughts, prayers, and what you learn from the Bible. This helps you remember and grow.
5. **Celebrate Your Commitment:** Whenever you pray the prayer of salvation, remember the joy in heaven, as described in Luke 15:10, because angels rejoice when someone repents and comes back to God.
6. **Keep Growing:** As you walk with Jesus, know that it's okay to take small steps. Allow Him to help you through life's ups and downs.

By taking these steps, you are not just starting a personal journey, but you are becoming part of God's family and embracing a life filled with love and purpose!

CHAPTER 7
Words of Encouragement

AS YOU START or continue your journey as a Kingdom Writer, I want to encourage and uplift you. Just like the prophets of old recorded their visions and dreams, your words can shine the light of truth and guidance for many. Stay committed to your writing and let your heart guide you. Remember what is written in Proverbs 16:3: "Commit your work to the Lord, and your plans will be established." The most powerful source of encouragement will always come from the Word of God. The Bible is not just something to read, it's a treasure to absorb and share creatively. Make it a habit to spend time in the Word, not only reading but also writing and speaking it over yourself. The Bible is vital to your calling as a writer. The verses flow both into you and out of you, nourishing and inspiring your heart and mind. Once you make God's Word a central part of your writing life, you'll realize just how much power you have to overcome challenges and shape your story through faith-filled words.

When you express yourself through writing, remember that as a Kingdom Writer, you should not remain silent when faced with challenges. God's Word is like a powerful sword, helping you fight against negativity and doubt. Just as Jesus used Scriptures to overcome temptation, you, too, have the power to use your words to shape your reality. Proverbs 18:21 reminds us, "The tongue can bring death or life; those who love to talk will reap the consequences." Realizing that your words have such amazing power is both a gift and a responsibility. Think about how you talk to yourself; it shapes who you are as a writer. Instead of saying things like, "I'm not a writer," try to express your faith: "I have the mind of Christ, and with the Holy Spirit's help, I will create works that inspire many to follow Jesus." Every word you speak helps define your story. As you understand this, you'll see that each positive affirmation sparks the creative gifts God has blessed you with. As you harness the power of positive words, it's equally important to be mindful of the thoughts you allow to shape your mindset and creativity.

It is important for Kingdom Writers to protect your thoughts and the messages you listen to. If you keep telling yourself you're not good enough, these thoughts will bleed into your writing. Instead, focus on the promises in Scripture that remind you of your true identity. Let your inner dialogue shift from doubt to reaffirming your calling. Change begins when God's Word replaces thoughts that bring you down with uplifting truths.

Many writers struggle with low self-esteem, often fearing that no one will care about their message. While not everyone will read your book, that's okay. What matters is obeying God's call to write. Ask yourself, "Has God called me to write?" Let the answers come from your relationship with Him, not from what others think. Seek the unique guidance that only God can provide about your writing journey.

Some writers even find it helpful to not just read the Bible, but to write it out, because it allows you to connect deeply with the text. Each time you write, you actively participate in God's story, planting seeds of His truth into your life and the lives of your readers. As you write, remember that you and your words are gifts. Each book you create can serve as a resource and a testimony of faith, so don't hesitate to share your story. Do not connect your call as a writer to what others think. Trust that God has a special path for you, and that your writing, inspired by Him, will touch those in need.

The world may try to intimidate you with doubts about your

abilities. But remember, you are not alone. Philippians 4:19 assures us, "And my God will supply all your needs according to his riches in glory in Christ Jesus." When you feel like giving up or when writing seems tough, know that God is there to support you. Each moment you stay true to your calling strengthens your reliance on Him.

When facing obstacles, remember that you can do all things through Christ who strengthens you (Philippians 4:13). Every writer's journey is different, and there's no need to compare yourself to others. Instead, joyfully embrace the way God has designed you to write. It's essential to honor your voice and cater to the specific audience God has prepared for your words. If you copy someone else, you might miss out on the special connections meant for you.

Let's remember an important truth from Acts 3:6: "But Peter said, 'I don't have any silver or gold for you. But I'll give you what I have. In the name of Jesus Christ the Nazarene, get up and walk!" This powerful reminder shows us that what we carry within us our faith, our testimony, and our words can be more valuable than anything material. Your words as a Kingdom Writer hold incredible value and purpose; they have the power to change lives, offer hope, and guide people toward God's wonderful love and truth.

Embrace your calling fully, understanding that it is a vital part of your unique journey and the impact you are meant to have. Even when you walk through tragedy or trauma, God can develop your greatest strengths from those experiences, equipping you to share, heal, and inspire others in ways you may not yet imagine. Every story you tell, every lesson you share, and every encouragement you offer can become a channel for God's love and healing, both for yourself and for those who read your words.

———

CHAPTER 7 SUMMARY: WORDS OF ENCOURAGEMENT FOR KINGDOM WRITERS

As you finish this book, remember that your journey as a writer is very special, especially if you see yourself as a Kingdom Writer. It's important to find encouragement in the Word of God, which is not just something we read, but something we can understand and live out. The words in the Bible are powerful for your calling and reading them can help you become a better writer and speaker.

When you write, keep in mind that your voice matters. Just like Jesus used Scripture to face tough times, you too can use God's Word to push away doubt and negativity. Proverbs 18:21 tells us that "the tongue has the power of life and death." Your words can shape who you are and how you feel about yourself. Instead of thinking, "I'm not a writer," try saying, "I can do this with God's help." Remember, every word you speak shapes your journey.

It's vital to take care of your thoughts. If you keep telling yourself you're not good enough, those feelings will show up in your writing. Instead, focus on what the Bible says about who you are. Shift your thoughts from feeling unsure to embracing your calling. When you replace negative thoughts with God's truths, you'll notice a difference.

Many writers have found it helpful to write out Bible verses. This helps them connect more deeply with God's messages. Every time you write, think of it as being part of God's story. Your books can inspire others and share your faith. Don't worry about what others think; trust that God has a unique path for you. Your writing can be a light that shows others the way to Christ.

Sometimes, it's easy to feel alone, but remember Philippians 4:19, which reminds us that God will meet all our needs. Keep going, especially when it feels hard. Your writing journey is yours, so don't compare it to anyone else's. Celebrate your unique voice and trust that God has a specific audience for your words.

ACTION STEPS

1. Spend time daily in the Bible to nourish your creativity.
2. Write out verses that speak to you and reflect on their meanings.
3. Affirm your identity as a child of God who is a Kingdom Writer with positive statements.
4. Focus on your unique voice and the message God has given you.
5. Share your story with others; it could light up someone's path.

Prayer

THE KINGDOM WRITER'S PRAYER

As I continue my journey as a Kingdom Writer, I look to God for direction, aiming to honor the promises He has made concerning my path. Each promise serves as a beacon, and I deliberately choose to personalize these affirmations, surrounding myself with visual reminders, notes pinned to my walls, verses written in my journal, and whispered truths that accompany me throughout my day.

These affirmations are vital, especially when I grapple with moments of uncertainty casting a shadow over my thoughts with questions like, "Why me, God?" In these times of doubt, I allow these sacred truths to resonate deeply within my spirit. I invite you to join me in this prayer to embrace these promises and strengthen our writing journeys together.

Father, in the name of Jesus,

I am reminded of Your words: "I knew you before I formed you as my writer in your mother's womb. Before you were born, I set you apart and appointed you as my prophet to the nations" (Jeremiah 1:5).

Lord, I am grateful that it is not I who chose You. You chose me, appointing me as a writer to go forth and produce lasting fruit, promising that whatever I ask in Your name, You will give me (John 15:16).

Help me, Lord, to reject the lies I tell myself. For I am Your chosen writer, a royal priest, and part of a holy nation, Your treasured possession. May I reflect Your goodness, having been called out of darkness into Your glorious light (1 Peter 2:9).

In times of trouble, teach me to see these challenges as opportunities for joy. Let my faith be tested, knowing that writing through these moments will develop my endurance. Allow me to embrace this growth, that I may be perfect and complete, lacking in nothing (James 1:2-4).

Remind me, Father, that my worth is not defined by the wisdom or wealth seen in this world. You have chosen what the world deems foolish to confound the wise (I Corinthians 1:26).

I place my trust in You fully, not relying on my understanding as I write. Guide me in all I do, revealing the path I should take (Proverbs 3:5-6).

May I one day confidently proclaim 2 Timothy 4:7-8, "I have fought the good fight, I have finished the race, I have remained faithful in my writing. And now, the prize awaits me, the crown of righteousness, which You, Lord, the righteous Judge, will give me on the day of Your return. And this prize is not just for me, but for all who eagerly await Your appearance."

Amen.

GET TO KNOW DOC

The author was interviewed by members of the Kingdom Writer Collaborative, a group designed to support both current and aspiring writers.

Question: If you could write anywhere in the world, where would that be?

> **Doc's Answer:** Oh, that's an easy one! My ideal writing space would be on a beautiful farm, in a room filled with books, a personal library, if you will. From my window, I would look out at the stunning beauty of nature that God has created, finding inspiration as I write my heart out unto the Lord. But in reality, I would probably be fussing at my grandson to stop chasing the dogs with the lawn mower and to quit coming in and out of my house, letting out all the cold air.

Question: If you could sit down with five people, past or present, who would they be, and what three questions would you ask?

> **Doc's Answer:** Well, to be honest, I wouldn't want to waste my first choice on a person. My first choice would be God. I have

three questions for Him: Before I ask any questions, thank you for all that you've done, and still do, walking with me on this journey of grief and writing. First, what is the real purpose of my writing? I want to understand what it is that I cannot see, a message that no one can tell me but You. Second, how are my husband and mom? I miss them dearly. I would then ask God if He could give them both a message for me. Third, I'd ask if He could set up a book signing in heaven so that when he calls me home, I could walk around and chat with all the authors of the Bible after He signs it first. That would be epic; I'd probably faint from excitement!

Next would be Jesus. I would be incredibly in awe to simply be in His presence. Once I gathered my thoughts, I would ask Him if I'm doing well, what I could improve during my time here, and if I am straying from my life's plan and purpose. I would seek any guidance or hints that might help me get back on track. And if it were possible, I would really like to give Him a long hug and stay in that moment as long as possible.

Next, I would talk to my mom. I'd want to thank her for everything she sacrificed for our family. I would ask if I could hug her and if her spirit could feel it because I just want her to hold me again. And then I'd lean in and say, "Girlfriend, tell me what heaven is like! I want the details that no one knows and hurry up because I don't know when God is sending me back, and I need the 411!"

Next, I would talk to my husband. I want to thank him for his sacrifices, love, wisdom, and leadership. If I could, I would hug him and kiss him on his forehead, just like he always kissed me. I would update him on the kids and his grandson. Then, I would tell him that it has been an honor to love him and to be loved by him. I also want him to know that I feel secure because he lived a life where he made sure we were okay. Tell him although I miss him dearly, Jesus has us, and we are good. Lastly, I would thank him for giving his life to Christ so that one day we could be together for all eternity.

I would then sit down with Wisdom. I would tell wisdom

that life is stressing me, and I'm trying to make it to that dinner party mentioned in Proverbs, but girl, the struggle is real! I do hear you, but sometimes I feel lost. My question for wisdom would be, can a truly wise person ever recognize their own wisdom?

I would love to ask the authors of the Bible how they stayed focused on writing their important books while facing tough times. If I could add one more person to my list, it would be C.S. Lewis. He is my favorite writer, and I would only ask him one question: What advice would you give me as a writer that you haven't shared in any of your books?

Sorry, that was more than five, lol.

Question: What are five things you would tell your younger self?

Doc's Answer: First off, stop trying to control everything! God has already laid out your life; you just need to wait for His cue, be obedient, and when He calls, be ready to play your part. Second, remember that life isn't guaranteed, you could go to sleep and wake up with the Lord. You will better understand later in life because that's how your mother and husband will eventually pass. Third, you are never truly alone. God is always with you, especially in those lonely times. Talk to Him often and stay in the Word. But even more importantly, never stop writing Scripture by hand; for you, it's a secret weapon in life. God has given you a gift not just to speak, but to write things into existence.

Don't forget to love others as well as yourself. And most crucially, remember those two lessons your mom and husband will repeatedly share with you: "Trust in the Lord (Trust the big man) with all your heart and lean not on your own understanding; in all your ways acknowledge Him, and He shall direct your paths." Always remember, "All you have is all you need."

Question: What are your five favorite books outside of the Bible?

Doc's Answer: I absolutely love *The Screwtape Letters* by C.S. Lewis, *The Richest Man in Babylon* by George Samuel Clayson, *Spiritual Leadership* by Oswald Sanders, *The 38 Letters from J.D. Rockefeller to His Son* by J.D. Rockefeller, and *Imagine Heaven* by John Burke. And yes, I love any memoirs or autobiographies as well because they are testimonies!

Question: Any words of wisdom for current and future writers?

Doc's Answer: Never change your message to cater to an ever-changing culture. The message—the Word of God—remains the same, even if the vehicle we use to deliver it is different.

Question: How do you pray for Kingdom Writers?

Doc's Answer: I pray for those who do and don't have a relationship with God, especially Kingdom Writers who are grappling with deliverance issues. I know that Satan thrives on blinding their minds. I often pray prayers that bind the enemy from their thoughts. As a matter of fact, I've prayed that, as they read this collection, God provides a protective barrier over them so there's no interference from the enemy. It has been a challenge for me because the enemy despises this, leading to constant spiritual attacks on my life. However, I find comfort in the fact that the Word is my weapon, and I have never lost a battle using it.

Question: Do you mind giving an example?

Doc's Answer: Sure, here is my prayer for deliverance.

In the mighty name of Jesus, I see you, Satan, relishing in the work of binding the minds of my fellow Kingdom Writers. I bind you from their minds and their entire being. From now on, the light shines, and they can see Jesus. I bind you, the enemy, and loose the light. Luke 10:2 says the harvest is great, but the workers are few. God, I pray that you order the steps of good, godly men and women across the paths of my fellow Kingdom Writers to encourage, teach, inspire, and activate the many blessings and gifts you have for them. Open their minds to receive the download you have for them to write. Let them see that it's bigger than any situation, greater than any life challenge, and that their calling is bigger than themselves. They are needed—I need them. But more importantly, you need them to fulfill your purpose and will. In the mighty name of Jesus, amen.

For those who maintain a relationship with Christ, I offer the prayer found in Ephesians 1:17-23 on their behalf. I ask for wisdom and revelation to deepen their understanding of Him, and that the eyes of their hearts may be opened and enlightened.

Question: What excuse bothers you the most about writers?

Doc's Answer: I view each person as a living book, eagerly waiting to be shared with the world. There's one excuse that truly unsettles me more than any other: the notion that your life is dull, and that no one would be interested in what you have to say. Well, let me tell you this: there is a whole community of people who might feel just as unexciting, and they too think that no one would be interested in what they have to say, and they need to hear your story. By sharing your experiences, you can come together to form a supportive community that transforms into an inspiring collective, eager to grow together with a shared love for Christ. In other words, stop making this excuse and just write!

Thanks

Thank You for Joining This Journey

Your story and your calling matter. If you found encouragement, clarity, or inspiration in these pages, I invite you to keep growing with our community of faith-driven writers.

Visit www.drcharisrooks.com to discover:

- **Mentorship & Coaching:** Personalized guidance for Christian writers at every stage, from first idea to published book.
- **Publishing Programs:** Step-by-step support to help you write, publish, and even launch your own publishing imprint.
- **The Kingdom Writer Collection:** Books, journals, and resources designed to equip and inspire you to fulfill your divine writing mission.
- **Workshops & Digital Resources:** Practical tools, digital planners, and exclusive content to help you grow your writing, your brand, and your ministry.
- **Free 30-Day Social Media Planner:** Sign up for our mailing list and receive a complimentary planner packed with Christ-centered content strategies and a ready-to-use posting calendar.

You're not alone on this path. Let's walk together, so your words can reach, heal, and impact the world.

Connect, learn more, and take your next step at www.drcharisrooks.com.